JESUS, TEACH US TO PRAY

Jerome Bertram

JESUS, TEACH US TO PRAY

IGNATIUS PRESS   SAN FRANCISCO

Cover art:
Stained glass window from
St Paul's Church, Walton Street, Oxford.
With kind permission of David Freud

Published in 2010 by Ignatius Press, San Francisco
ISBN 978-1-58617-428-6
Library of Congress Control Number 2009935365
Printed in the United States of America ♾

Contents

Forethought

"My house shall be called a house of prayer", says the Lord (Matth. 21:13). If the greatest work of a Christian is prayer, one of the greatest responsibilities of a priest must be to teach the people to pray, as Our Lord taught His disciples. Years of attempts to do that, and responses from so many students, parishioners, and penitents, have been a slight preparation for this audacious undertaking. More proximate preparations have been the retreat conferences inflicted on various communities in 2006 and 2007: the Benedictine sisters of St Mildred at Minster in Thanet; the proto-Oratorian ordinands at "Stepaside" near George at the foot of the Outiniqua pass; the white black-monks of Prinknash. Most of this was first written in Port Elizabeth in the house of the Oratorian community in formation in the autumn of 2007. On returning to Europe I found that, as so often happens with me, someone else had been writing on the same subject. In this case it was the Pope. Reading *Jesus of Nazareth* reassured me about much that I had written already, but provided extraordinary new insights which I have unashamedly incorporated into this re-written text.

For all those, therefore, who have wittingly or un-wittingly contributed, many thanks, and one request, "as you from crimes would pardoned be, let your indulgence set me free."

Jerome Bertram, Oxford

7

—·•·—

CHAPTER I

Why Pray?

Before we can talk about how to pray, we must first wonder why we pray at all – what is the point of it? Why do so many people set aside time every day to pray, why are there professionals, monks and nuns, whose whole lives revolve around prayer?

There are two wrong answers, commonly held, and one which I think is the right answer. The wrong answers, the misunderstandings, can bring the whole of our Christian faith into disrepute. What I propose to set forth as the right answer is, I trust, one that might recommend the faith to those who have rejected it because of the misunderstandings. The two wrong answers are these: (one) the purpose of prayer is to make God give us things; and (two) the purpose of prayer is to give us an inner experience. What I believe to be the true purpose of prayer is this: to open our hearts to the love of God, so that love can flow through us to other people.

Forcing God to do our will

I suppose the most common misapprehension of prayer is that it is just asking for things. On that basis, if we ask things for ourselves it can be selfish, but if we ask things for other people, it is charitable. When they hear that Christians spend long hours in prayer, many people imagine that all they are doing is reciting immensely long lists of the things they want, and the names of the people they would like to do well, and giving God detailed instructions on how to put right everything that is wrong with his world. It is not only the ignorant who think this is what prayer means. Learned historians writing about the mediaeval Church seem to imagine that monks and chantry priests spent their day wheedling God to be nice to the people who were paying for their upkeep, and telling God over and over again what their names are, and what they would like for Christmas. That provides a handy excuse for despising the foolishness of mediaeval Christians, and therefore of modern Catholic Christianity. Maybe that is why, these days, it is historians more often than scientists who ridicule Catholicism, at least in the popular media.

That is the prayer of a child, and a badly instructed child at that. If we think of prayer as simply demanding things from God there are two immediate consequences. One is that it totally eliminates any idea of love, for how can you say you love someone if your entire conversation with them consists of relentless demands? The other is that it clearly doesn't work. God does not immediately give us everything we demand, no matter how many times we demand it.

So we may move on to a slightly more subtle approach, especially if we have opened a book of prayers and seen what it contains. God, we imagine, needs to be flattered, so we ply him with prayers of praise and thanksgiving. The long and complicated texts of the liturgy are, we imagine, particularly amusing in God's eyes; he has a special delight in sixteenth-century English prose style, and if we perform it beautifully he will be so charmed that he will, after all, give us what we demand. The more subtle historians have discovered that the prayers said by mediaeval monks were not just lists of demands, but consisted of the psalms, hymns and canticles of the Divine Office, but maybe we think these are just what God needs in order to be inclined to listen to our requests. Visitors to modern monasteries make the same discovery, they find that the long prayers of the monks consist largely of these texts from Scripture, and contain very few direct requests, but this, they conclude, must be the most effective way of lulling God into a good mood.

Can anyone really have such a childish view of God? And is it not obvious that this approach is still totally devoid of love? If our relationship with one we claim to love consists of nothing but attempts to amuse him, with the sole purpose of persuading him to give us something, can we really call that love? For that matter, it still doesn't work, though if we are praying for the souls of the dead we have no way of knowing that it doesn't work. That gives the sceptics an excuse to claim that the whole purpose of building churches and the system of endowing chantries and monasteries has never been more than a cynical plot to extract money from the laity to keep the clergy in comfort. (Assuming that getting up at three in the morning to sing psalms for two hours is what you call comfort.)

The problem with the sceptics is that they are incapable of imagining that anyone would ever do anything except for selfish reasons. And as long as we think that prayer is a means of getting our own will, we are reinforcing their delusions.

A particularly pernicious variation on the theme of prayer as a means of forcing God to do our will is the obsession with particular forms and times of prayer. Experience shows that simply demanding things from God doesn't work, and it still doesn't work if we try to make our demands less rude by covering them with praise and thanks, so the conclusion is that we have not been saying the prayers in quite the correct form. For this reason people compose weird and wonderful forms of prayer, with instructions that they must be recited in precisely the right tone of voice, the right number of times, on precisely the right days, facing the right direction. And they feel obliged to leave a set number of copies of these strange incantations lying around in churches on a set number of particular days, or paying to have them inserted into undiscriminating newspapers. All with the proviso that you must be quite sure you really want what you are asking for, because if you fulfil all these conditions it will certainly be granted. Clergy have to be on the watch for these "junk prayers" and remove them promptly from the church, because they are, really, a form of blasphemy. They are attempts to make God do tricks, to force Him to obey us by carrying out a special ritual which He is unable to resist.

It is, of course, sheer paganism. According to the ancient poets, like Homer, the fickle and unpredictable gods of the pagans can be cajoled, threatened, bribed or blackmailed into doing our will, and if all else fails you can set one god off against another. Even in classical Rome the rituals of their religion were laid down in the greatest detail, and if you failed to carry them out exactly and precisely as ordained, the whole ceremony would have to begin all over again, otherwise the sun would not rise, and the spring would not come. The prophet Elijah makes fun of this pagan concept in his famous encounter with the priests of Baal. (I Kings 18:20-40) "Cry aloud," he taunts them, "for he is a god; either he is musing, or he has gone aside, or he is on a journey, or perhaps he is asleep and must be awakened." They limped and raved around their altars from morning to night, and there was no answer. Elijah's prayer is not like that: he calls on the true God with absolute confidence. Paganism goes with magic: magic is the attempt to gain power over spirits and force them to do our will, through various rites which they are unable to resist. It simply can't be done. There may be various blind forces of nature, "elementary beings which by nature are not gods", (Gal. 4:8) which might possibly be manipulated in some way, but no intelligent being can be forced to do our will by any amount of dancing, chanting or burning of strange substances. Still less can God be trained to our command: He is not a tame lion.

You cannot force anyone to love you. Not even an animal can be forced to love you. God cannot even force you to love Him. Love must be free, otherwise it is no love. The horrid old stories about using philtres to force people to fall in love with each other all end in disaster. If our relationship with God is not about love, then it is nothing. Prayer must not be seen as a complicated means of getting our own way.

Sublimated selfishness

There is another common misconception of prayer, which has attracted much attention from the learned, and has even, it appears, taken in many professed religious. It is that prayer is about gaining an inner experience, which enables us to realise our true selves. What this inner experience consists of, is difficult to say. Some see it as inner peace, or tranquillity; the mastery of one's own desires and appetites, the ability to control one's thoughts and emotions. Others see it in more nihilist term as the quest for nothingness, the still centre of the turning world, without thoughts, without words, without action. Comparative anthropologists scan the pages of the mystics of all "traditions" attempting to find the common element which is the essence of religion, convinced that all the "higher" or "classic" religions are aiming at the same experience. Convents and monasteries advertise "retreats" with the declared aim of helping us build up our inner selves, realise our true potentials, and incidentally help our companies to become more efficient and therefore more profitable.

I am not going to examine non-Christian traditions here, they must defend themselves. All I can say is that the whole Christian tradition of spiritual writing is utterly opposed to this goal of self-perfection, this ideal of building up myself. "He must increase," said John the Baptist, "but I must decrease." (John 3:30) The Christian mystic seeks to become smaller, not greater, to surrender myself to God, not to become His equal, to hand over control to Him, not to assert it for myself. The Christian mystic, above all, does not want to look at nothingness but to look at Him who is everything, not towards the sublime but towards the incarnate, to direct the gaze away from self towards the Word made Flesh. The goal is to strike out this "I" that keeps intruding into our conversation, to put a line through it, and so make a cross.

All this talk of developing the inner self is just a more refined form of selfishness. Instead of demanding money or women or slaves, we demand knowledge and power. We apply for admission to the exquisite and transcendent inner circle of those who really know, those who are in touch with the universe. Oh, it can all sound very splendid, but it is just as sordid and selfish as the Christmas list sort of prayer, and far less honest. What is more, all too quickly it comes back to the elementary demands, building up one's strength of character in order to make ourselves irresistible to women, cultivating the inner tranquillity in order to increase business. A lot of those "mystical inner secrets" turn out to be pretty vulgar after all.

False spirituality is deceptive, because it uses the language of real spirituality. Moreover the effects it claims to produce, the inner tranquillity and self-control, are by-products of genuine prayer. Again, we only have to think of the parallels in human love. If we really love someone, he certainly will give us good things, including the little toys which the sublimely exquisite may affect to despise, but these are not the purpose for which we love him – we love Him for His own sake, or love is not love. We may feel we have risen above making endless demands on our beloved's generosity, but if our motive in loving Him is to make ourselves feel good, we cannot call that love. True love does make us feel good, but only because that is not what we are aiming at. The love of God gives us everything precisely because we do not demand anything.

True love of God and neighbour

To get away from the miasma of false speculations we need nothing more than the simple words of Scripture: Our Lord's great new commandment is simply this, "love one another as I have loved you." (John 15:12-17) If we know how much God loves us, then we shall be able to love others, for "love is of God, and he who loves is born of God and knows God … . No man has ever seen God; if we love one another God abides in us and his love is perfected in us." (I John 4:7-11) All prayer, all worship, is an attempt to fulfil the greatest commandment, "you shall love the Lord your God with all your heart, and with all your soul, and with all your might." (Deut. 6:5) If you do that, then you will find yourself constrained, almost forced to "love your neighbour as yourself" (Matt. 22:36-40), because "Christ's love constrains us". (II Cor. 5:14 Nicholas King version – the RSV won't do here. Maybe "spurs us on", *urget nos*)

I propose to take it as axiomatic that we are put on this earth in order to learn how to love. That begins with the love of God, and must develop into the love of neighbour. We can learn nothing except by practising, and our knowledge increases as we tackle more and more difficult exercises. It is necessary sometimes for God to pretend to be difficult to love; neighbours can be difficult without pretending. That is why growth in the love of God comes during the difficult times, when prayer seems dry and tedious; growth in the love of neighbour comes when God confronts us with more and more difficult people to love.

The definition of prayer that I offer is this: prayer is an opening of heart and soul and might to absorb the love of God, to allow Him to irradiate us with His love, to soak into us so that we are saturated with a love that must overflow and radiate outwards towards those we meet. In the process we will become aware of His overwhelming love for us, a love that builds us up, burns away all our defects, transforms us into precisely the sort of person we most want to be. It is true, then, that prayer does enhance us, but only if we begin on the road of opening outwards towards love. If our intention is our own gain, we shall succeed in gaining nothing. If our intention is to turn outwards to God and neighbour, then we shall discover how much we have gained in the process, not less than everything.

In this, it is exactly like married human love, which is why that is the perfect parable for the love of God. (Eph. 5:32) If our intention is simply to use a spouse as a means of enhancing our own life, we shall fail in misery. If our whole delight is in the happiness of the spouse, we shall find that our own life has been transformed and fulfilled. Moreover, once we are transformed in love, we shall discover that we have everything we could possibly want. Of course many of the things we thought we wanted turn out to be childish toys that we no longer care for, but once we are perfected in love, why then "You cannot now cherish a wish which ought not to be wish'd." (Newman, *Dream of Gerontius*)

How long does all this take? At least one lifetime. Indeed they are fortunate who complete it in this life, which is why for most of us the ultimate purging experience of the love of God comes after death. But we can make a good start now. What else is life for?

Prayer of Intercession

Does all this mean that we should never ask for anything in prayer, either for ourselves or for others? By no means, that would be to contradict the entire tradition of the Church as well as the plain recommendation of Our Lord. We are encouraged to lay our needs before God, and to commend to Him those we love, even more so those we have failed to love. But all our prayers of petition must be

made with the proviso, "Not as I will but as Thou wilt."
(Matth. 26:39)

When we pray for ourselves, we should be thinking
of our real needs, which are spiritual; we should pray
earnestly for "love, joy, peace, patience, kindness,
goodness, faithfulness, gentleness, self-control". (Gal.
5:22-23) These are things which every one of us should
want, which all of us can use. We should be praying
also for the gifts which enable us to build up Christ's
Church, not excluding wisdom, knowledge, faith, gifts
of healing, the working of miracles, prophecy, the
discernment of spirits and even the gift of tongues.
(Cf. I Cor 12:8-11) These, commonly called "charisms",
are the heritage of the whole Church, distributed by
the Holy Spirit to particular people, different ones for
different workers in the Lord's vineyard, but they are
often given for a specific time and withdrawn when they
are no longer needed.

Above all others, there are the three things that last,
"faith, hope, and love, but the greatest of these is love".
(I Cor. 13:13) If we open our hearts to love, which I
have taken to be the definition of prayer, we are opening
them to all the good things that God wants to bestow
on us. These are things we certainly should pray for, and
which in due time God will certainly grant. We may think
we can set our own timetable, and pray for "patience,
immediately", or even, like St Augustine, for "chastity,
but not yet", (*Confessions*, VIII, 7) but God has His own
timetable: He may grant one virtue straight away, and ask
us to wait most of our life for another. One of His gifts

is the ability to be patient with our own failings. (Cf. II Cor. 12:9) And all the gifts include with them the gift of happiness in this world, which comes from knowing the love of God.

Happiness, or Christian joy, is one of the characteristics the Church looks for in discerning who can be called a saint. Yet appearances can be deceptive. Blessed Teresa of Calcutta seemed to radiate joy around her, but as we know from her writings, that surface of joy overlaid a deep layer of sorrow, a sharing in the suffering of Christ which she was only able to accept after many years of suffering. Deep, deep within her was the heart of glory, which enabled her to persevere in her mission, a glory which was concealed from her during her lifetime, but visible to everyone else. There have been many saints who have been remarkable for the appearance of joy, St Philip Neri in particular, but joy, and even glory, are not incompatible with sorrow, as long as that sorrow is an accepted share in the compassion of Christ for suffering humanity.

We pray in particular, then, for spiritual things. Can we pray for material things as well? Yes, but not in the same way. It is a natural instinct to ask God for health, good weather, deliverance from danger, and so on, but we should not go on about it. It is enough simply to mention these things in our prayers. In the same way when we pray for other people, we do not need to waste time in our prayer telling God all about our friends, their illnesses, their employment opportunities, their exams. It is enough simply to think of their names, to pray "for all those who in general or in particular have asked my prayers".

A common problem during community prayer, or when priests rashly invite the people to contribute "spontaneous bidding prayers", is that people stand up and compose long prayers which begin with a description of the problems that worry them ("as you will have read in today's paper, O Lord, there has been another earthquake in China ...") and then go on to moralise for the benefit of those who overhear them ("help us to be aware that by our support for corrupt and incompetent politicians we are directly contributing to the suffering of people in poor countries...") before giving God the answer to His problems, ("help us to put pressure on the government and the United Nations to establish peace and democracy in all lands"). That is not a prayer: it is a political speech. Prayer should be, "O Lord, we pray for those suffering in China and elsewhere." That is enough: God knows the situation better than we do, and He knows the solution. Though, if our prayer really is an opening to the love of God, He might even give us the grace to become His agent in relieving suffering.

When we pray for others, our intention must always be for whatever is really best for them, not what we think is good for them, or even what they might fancy they want. "Thy choicest gifts in store, on her be pleased to pour" is actually rather a good prayer. Leave it to God to decide what is best. "Father, what you buy me I like best". (GM Hopkins, *The Handsome Heart*) All we need do in our prayer is to make an act of love for those we care about, and join ourselves to them before God. It doesn't matter if they are aware of this or not. There will be many surprises when the Books are opened, and we discover how much we have been helped by the quiet prayers of someone we were hardly aware of, or even of how much our prayers have been helping someone we lost touch with years ago. Exactly the same principle applies in our prayers for the dead: we commend them to the love of God, and our gift of love joins with the love of God in cleansing them from the woes of this world and making them fit for eternal happiness. We shall find out in due course what the effect of our prayers has been!

CHAPTER II

In the Upper Room

There are so many questions about prayer, and we cannot often find simple answers. Should we keep our prayers to ourselves, or should we look for companions? Should we pray alone indoors, "in our private room", or in church, in the open air, at the street corners? Should we pray morning and night, or midday, or when? When we do find the answers, they can be surprising.

Our companions in Prayer

The very earliest description of the Church is found in the Acts of the Apostles (1:13-14). "They went up to the upper room where they were staying, Peter and John and James and Andrew, Philip and Thomas, Bartholomew and Matthew, James the son of Alphaeus and Simon the Zealot and Judas of James. All these with one accord devoted themselves to prayer, together with the women and Mary the mother of Jesus, and with his brethren."

23

To be authentic to the scriptural model, therefore, prayer should be made in the upper room, in company with the apostles, the brethren, the women, and Mary. We cannot pray alone: whenever and wherever we pray, we pray always in that company, whether we are aware of them or not. All prayer is made through the Church, for the Church is the body of Christ present in this world, and outside that body we have no contact with the Father. "God desires all men to be saved, and to come to the knowledge of the truth. For there is one God, and there is one mediator between God and man, the man Christ Jesus." (I Tim. 2:4-5) All prayer is made through the Holy Spirit, for it is the Spirit of the Father and the Son who breathes within us, when we pray as members of the Body of Christ to the Father whom He came to reveal. "The Spirit helps us in our weakness; for we do not know how to pray as we ought, but the Spirit himself intercedes for us with sighs too deep for words." (Rom. 8:26)

That does not mean, of course, that we have to be conscious of the fact: there are uncounted millions who pray devoutly to the Eternal Father without realising that their prayer is only possible because the Word was made Flesh, humanity has been joined to the divine, and our little lives are caught up into the life of God. The Incarnation is of benefit to the entire human race, even to those who may think they are very far from the Faith, through misunderstanding or prejudice or simple ignorance.

The biologists tell us that no one can live without oxygen, and that our life is utterly dependent on a regular supply. For millions of years people managed to breathe very happily without knowing that, and there must be plenty of people alive now who have never heard of oxygen, but they survive, and they do not all suffocate. Nor do we call the biologists "intolerant" or "prejudiced" when they tell us that oxygen is necessary to our life, and they in turn do not deny that people can still breathe without knowing about it. In exactly the same way, when we affirm that all prayer, all the soul's health, comes through Jesus Christ and none other, we are not claiming that those who do not know about Him cannot pray. When they pray they are unconsciously breathing His spirit, just as those ignorant of biology unconsciously breathe oxygen. What we do claim and maintain, despite hostility and persecution is that "there is no other name under heaven through which man can be saved." (Acts 4:12) People cannot be saved *through* a false religion, but they can be saved *despite* their false religion, and through those elements of truth that they do know. For Truth is not an abstraction – Truth is a person, and His name is Jesus.

Every human being, from the sheer fact of being human, has a link to the Father because the Son of God shares our human nature. So we are all His brethren. In the very next verse of the Acts of the Apostles after the one we opened with (Acts 1:15) we are told that the "brethren" numbered one hundred and twenty, ordinary disciples of Christ (of both sexes) as opposed to the twelve chosen Apostles, and the inner group of holy women. The number of brethren expanded very rapidly, to the thousands who listened to the first preaching

(Acts 2:41) and the tens of thousands who formed the first churches throughout the Mediterranean world. St Paul extends the word to the entire human race: we are all brethren, "for we are indeed his offspring". (Acts 17:28)

The only thing that could block our prayer would be a deliberate, conscious, decision to exclude our "brethren". Obviously we need not be particularly conscious of our solidarity with the entire human race as a precondition for prayer; but we should not consciously isolate ourselves from them. The old pagan philosopher Plotinus might have babbled about the "flight of the alone to the Alone", but that is not Christian prayer: ours is the flight of the many to the Three in One. We are not alone, any more than God is alone. Whether we are praying in a crowded township teeming with humanity, or in the most remote part of the karoo with limitless empty space all around us, our prayer is always supported by the brethren, and in union with them, those we can see, and those we cannot see. In fact it can be very much easier to be conscious of our love and association for other people when they are not too close around us: some people are best loved at a distance.

We pray together with the Apostles. St Luke gives us the names, the list of the Twelve, as he did in the Gospel (Luke 6:14-16), though one is missing. We have met these eleven characters before, in the stories about the life and death of Jesus; some are more familiar than others, most are in some way or other disreputable. These too must be the companions of our prayer. We cannot exclude the coward Peter, the foolish Thomas, the braggart sons of Zebedee, or even the obscure Jude. The Church was founded on those twelve men precisely because they were so very ordinary, undistinguished, weak and quarrelsome. If we fancy we are in any way superior to them, we have no chance of learning to pray. The only difference between the eleven who survived, and the one who did not, is that the eleven were prepared to admit their weaknesses, accept their own failings, and cry out in repentance, "Lord, you know everything, you know that I love you." (John 21:17)

And more to the point, we pray together with them precisely because they are the foundation stones of the Church. (Apoc. 21:14) All are rocks, but Peter in particular is the Rock on which Christ built His Church. (Matth. 16:18) He is the leader and spokesman for them all. His ministry is not separate from that of the others, but it does not depend on them either. When he speaks, he speaks with the authority of God, as the Scripture shows us: "flesh and blood has not revealed this to you, but my Father who is in heaven". (Matth. 16:17) Again, it is not necessary to know this, and many pray devoutly in blissful ignorance, or so afflicted by prejudice that they are effectively unable to recognise the truth. Their prayer is valid, and the love of God flows freely into their lives, because the only thing that can block our prayer is a wilful refusal to accept the Church that Christ founded, if we once know that it is founded on the Rock.

We pray together with the women. Throughout the Gospels we are reminded of the group of devout women who followed Jesus from Galilee, and looked after Him. They were the ones who stood near the Cross, when nearly all the men had run away; they were the ones who went to the tomb in the early morning, and found it empty; they heard the angels, they were the first to bring the good news of the Resurrection. Mary the mother of James and Joset, Mary of Cleopas, Salome, Joanna, Susanna, Martha and Mary Magdalen; they are the witnesses to the truth, they form the body of the Church, they give scope to the ministry of the apostles. From the beginning until now it seems the majority of people in our churches have been women, and it is they who are responsible for passing on the message from generation to generation. Almost all of us first heard the name of Jesus from our mother, and she from her mother, and so back to the witness of those first women at the empty tomb. And what our mothers did not tell us we learnt from nuns and other women teachers. Our prayer has to include them all.

And of all women in particular we pray with Mary, the mother of Jesus. If we drive her away, how can we expect her Son to stay with us? For she is the ideal model for all our prayer: "behold the handmaid of the Lord, be it done unto me according to thy Word." (Luke 1:38) Unless we can echo that prayer, we cannot be saved, for the whole of our faith depends on openness and submission to the Will of God.

All the world waited, poised to hear Mary's reply to the angel. The whole history of creation has been building up to this moment; all of the Old Testament is a preparation for her response. God's chosen people have been brought out of Ur of the Chaldees, out of Egypt, across the Red Sea, into the Promised Land, so that they should begin to be a people consecrated to God. Through centuries the prophets called them, cajoled them, denounced them, encouraged them, until slowly, little by little, they learnt what God's purposes were, the salvation of the whole of humanity through Israel. One tribe was set aside and made holy; one family in that tribe prepared and instructed, until at last a child could be born, "chosen before the creation began", and preserved from the ancient inheritance of sin and ignorance. Now her moment has come: she is asked to undertake the crucial role, she is asked to be the one in whom heaven and earth are to be united. She represents the whole of humanity, poised, ready to be caught up into that unique union of creator and creature which was God's purpose from the beginning.

It was God's purpose, His initiative. It is only by His grace that Mary had been brought to this point. We must not imagine that Gabriel had selected her at random, and could have gone on round the village to find someone else if she had not been at home. She was called because she was the one already chosen. Mary was not chosen because she was good – she was good because she was chosen. But she had the freedom to accept her vocation, or to reject it. Creation waited for her answer, for if she were to choose wrongly, it is beyond our calculation how long we should have had to wait for another opportunity.

(See St Bernard, Sermon IV on the Virgin Mother, quoted in the Office of Readings for 20th December.)

Her glory, and our salvation, depends on her consent, "let it be done unto me according to thy Word". And so she agreed to co-operate in our redemption, representing all of us in her acceptance of the divine into humanity.

Our Lady, we are told more than once, "pondered these things in her heart". The heart, in Biblical language, signifies more than just emotion: it is used as a symbol of purpose, will and direction, as well as understanding. That means that she thought about the astonishing things that were happening round her, she related them to what she already knew of God, she understood how everything fitted together with God's purposes, she united her will with those purposes and rejoiced in that union of heart and will between her and God. And because of that union, she was aware that "henceforth all generations will call me blessed". (Luke 1:48) That is why we speak of the Immaculate Heart of Mary as a model for ourselves. We too are to ponder God's ways, and unite our intentions to His. In that lies our freedom, and therefore our joy. If we are restricted by ignorance and sin, we are not totally free to breathe with the Spirit of God, to unite our wills to Him. Our Lady alone had that perfect freedom; our freedom is restricted, but the more we try to match our intentions to the will of God, the greater will be our genuine freedom. Prayer is the means by which we grow into that perfect freedom of the children of God, to share the life of Our Lady and the other saints.

Praying to or with the Saints

When we talk about praying *with* the saints, is that the same thing as praying *to* them? What does it mean to speak of prayer to Our Lady or a saint? Many people still imagine that we treat them as alternatives to God, and it is true that a superficial look at some prayer texts, or the behaviour of some people in front of statues, can give a very strange impression.

There is perhaps a little confusion in the English language, as it has developed over the last few centuries. It is worth digressing a little, because people delight in deliberately misrepresenting our use of the words "pray" and "worship". The word "pray" originally meant simply to "ask", so that you would "pray" the butcher to give you a leg of mutton, you would "pray" your friends to put in a good word for you when they met the Mayor, you would "pray" Our Lady to "pray" for you before God. Nineteenth-century historical novelists were fond of the word "prithee" (I pray thee) to mean "please". Only in the twentieth century did the word "pray" become narrowed in scope to mean the lifting up of heart and mind to God (a meaning formerly expressed by the word "orison"). Now that its meaning has become so precise, it is perhaps no longer quite appropriate to talk about "praying" to the saints, any more than we pray to our friends on earth. Certainly when we talk about "prayer" meaning mental prayer or contemplation, we cannot imagine using it except when we mean prayer in union with God.

In a very similar way the word "worship" has become narrower in meaning. In the past it simply meant "honour", so you talked of the "Worshipful Company of Butchers", or "his Worship the Mayor". Theologians made a clear distinction in Latin between *latria*, the honour paid only to God the Creator, and *doulia*, the human honour paid to the saints (and for that matter the mayor). Even in the nineteenth century the word was still slightly ambiguous, but nowadays the English word "worship" has come to mean exclusively *latria*, it means the supreme honour we give to God alone. In the modern sense of the word the Catholic Church has never for one moment tolerated the idea of "worshipping" anyone other than God, and it is dishonest to quote late mediaeval sources using the word "worship" in the old sense, in an attempt to prove that she ever did.

Our attitude towards the saints, the holy men and women who have gone before us, is that we respect them, and honour them as outstanding examples of what the grace of God can do in a soul that really opens to the action of love. This may also include profiting from their example, or from their surviving writings. For instance, we respect St Thérèse of Lisieux for what she wrote, we respect Blessed Teresa of Calcutta for what she did. In both cases we may feel moved to involve them consciously in our prayer, wanting to associate ourselves with their attitude of love and openness to God, their acceptance of difficulties in faith, their compassion with those who suffer. That is really what we mean when we say, aloud or in silence, "Saint Thérèse, Blessed Teresa, pray for me!"

We know that they are very special, and feel confident that with their prayers joined to ours we can more easily open ourselves to the love of God.

In exactly the same way, of course, we ask our living friends to pray for us. If we are anxious or in difficulties it is the most natural instinct to ask for the prayers of others, and to promise them that we will pray for them. Our solidarity with the rest of the Church means that we need never pray alone – in fact we cannot pray alone. Whether we know it or not, all our prayer is in union with the "saints", meaning both those alive now on earth, and those who have gone before us. Sometimes we like to be conscious of the fact, to remember that our favourite aunt in Australia has promised to pray for us, and to remember that our favourite saint in Heaven can also be relied on to pray for us. Neither our earthly friends nor our heavenly ones can actually grant prayers: only God can do that. Nor can they be fused with us in the loving embrace of contemplative union, that is something we aspire to in God alone. But they pray with us, and for us, and we need not be ashamed to ask their prayers.

In the Upper Room

We pray, therefore, in union with Our Lady and the Apostles, with all the saints, and all the sinners who make up the Body of Christ. If we are aware of that communion, our prayer can be so much easier, for we become aware that ours is just one voice in a vast chorus of triumphant praise, and if for a few bars we pause to draw breath, who will notice the pause, while the song continues around us? Being aware of the Church praying with us means that we need not be afraid if we find it difficult to pray at any particular time, whether we are ill or tired or out of sorts – the chorus roars on around us. And when we are feeling strong and tuneful, our voice may help cover up for someone gasping for breath the other side of the world. We never pray alone, it is not up to me on my own to make my lone voice heard in heaven, for I have tens of thousands of companions on either side to support me, just as Moses was supported in his prayer by Aaron and Hur. (Exodus 17:8-13)

Wherever we pray is the "upper room". Sometimes we have the opportunity to choose our place of prayer, some leafy bower in a green countryside, or the vast expanse of the open desert, beneath the sombre arches of an ancient church, or in the frivolous swirl of a Baroque basilica. Or we may find that our prayer is best in the sordid surroundings of a bed-sitting room in the crowded suburb, or wedged upright in a swaying underground train on the way to work. Whether humanity presses close around us, or we are isolated and away from everyone, whether our surroundings are beautiful and poetic, or humdrum and squalid, wherever we are, we can pray. And that place is the upper room.

Of course the style and manner of our prayer will be very different depending on where we are – we shall come to that. But it will be genuine prayer if we know that we are together with the saints in the upper room. Why is that? It is because the Upper Room was the place where the Lord took bread and broke it, and said "this is my Body". Our prayer is, above all, a eucharistic prayer, because our union with the Apostles and saints, and with all sinners throughout the world, is a union formed by communion. By sharing in the Body of Christ we become the Body of Christ.

That is the answer to the question of how we are able to make contact with those who have died – it is through Holy Communion. When we receive Holy Communion, we are united to Jesus Christ. But in that common union, we are also linked to everyone else who is united to Him. We cannot keep Him to ourselves. The saints in heaven are those who have achieved that union with the Divine which is the purpose of our existence. We have therefore a link to each of them through the Blessed Sacrament, and in no other way. That does not only mean the canonised, publicly recognised, saints, like Padre Pio or St Philip Neri; it includes the countless unrecognised holy men and women through the ages, among whom we can surely count personal friends. We may feel conscious of our union with them (though it is more likely we shall not), but that doesn't stop them being part of that great chorus of praise.

Our union with those we love on earth is achieved in exactly the same way – that aunt in Australia is united to Christ when she receives Holy Communion, we are united to Him when we receive Communion, and so we are united to each other across the curve of the earth. Even those kneeling next to us in church are more closely united to us, and therefore praying in closer union with us, when we have both received the Body of Christ together.

It is well for us if we are conscious of this, aware of the immense privilege of being members of the visible Body of Christ, the Church, in this life. But our common humanity extends to those who are unaware of it: their prayer is the prayer of the Church precisely because the Church, formed by the Eucharist, is diffused throughout the world. The grace they receive is a grace of the Church, because it is in the Church that Christ remains present in the world. Nowhere in the world can you be very far from a Catholic altar, where the Blessed Sacrament is reserved, and where Mass is celebrated. No one in the world is at more than two removes from personal acquaintance with a communicating Catholic. The love of God made flesh suffuses the whole of our world, and the entire human race, even though three quarters of us may be blissfully unaware of it.

Prayer can only be blocked if we deliberately and consciously thrust the Body of Christ away from us. The wilful refusal to accept what we know to be true is the ultimate blasphemy, the sin against the Holy Spirit. That is why truth, integrity, is so important, in prayer and also in the approach to the sacraments. It is a lie against supreme Truth if we try to snatch the Eucharistic Body while rejecting and spurning the Mystical Body. There are many who still perceive Truth in a different way, but if they are honest in their quest for it, passionate about the Truth, they are truly looking for Christ even though they do not know it. They will certainly find Him, or rather He will have found them. The only thing that can prevent that is if they positively refuse to want to know the Truth, or make a superficial demand for Christ without His Church. Accepting the Body of Christ must mean accepting Him in His Church, the whole jack, joke, poor potsherd, patch, matchwood hotchpotch of sinners who accept His Body in the hope of becoming saints. As long as we even faintly desire to wish to want to be in that number, then our prayer will be open to the love of God, and in due time, or out of time, He will lead us to be conscious of the wholeness of His love for us all.

CHAPTER III

Talking with God

The remarks in the first chapter about the misuse of set words in prayer must not for a moment be understood as implying that we should not use words, including repeated set prayers, and liturgical forms. As the poet remarked, "I've gotta use words when I talk to you" (TS Eliot, *Sweeney Agonistes*), and for most of the time we all need to use words in talking to God. But we use words for our benefit, not for His.

Vocal private Prayer

Our first prayers are almost certainly going to be the Our Father, and the Hail Mary. They will also, we hope, be our last prayers, "at the hour of our death". Never can we do without them, even if the remainder of our prayer is silent. Those two basic Catholic prayers are always going to be part of our life. To them, as we grow up, we add the other well-known Catholic prayers, the Glory Be, the Hail Holy Queen, the Memorare, the Morning Offering, the Act of Contrition, the Apostles' Creed. We shall discover others, and add them to our collection of favourites. These are what a child means by "saying prayers", and that is how we all have to begin. We shall and should progress to other types of prayer, but it would be very perilous ever to imagine that we are too grown-up to say our prayers "like a little child".

After those basic prayers, the use of words, "vocal prayer", comes in an extraordinary variety of forms. It makes a huge difference whether we are praying with other people, in the home, in church, or elsewhere, or whether we are alone, in silence, or aloud, speaking or singing. No particular type of prayer is "right" for all occasions, or for all people. The one fundamental rule of prayer, which I am liable to repeat over and over again, is "pray as you can and don't try to pray as you can't." (This is the refrain of many of Abbot Chapman's *Spiritual Letters*.)

Talking with God is not unlike talking with other people, in our use of words. We do not confine our conversation to the simple transfer of information. Many of us talk to our friends incessantly, saying nothing in particular, and not really listening to what each other are saying, but communicating our friendship just by the torrent of syllables. It is a rare friendship that is relaxed enough for both to remain in silence for any length of time, though we shall come to that. Many of the words we use have no real meaning at all, like "bye-bye", but we know what we mean by them. (Yes, yes, I know it is short for "goodbye" which originally meant "God be with you", but hardly anybody is conscious of that when they say "bye-bye".) We can convey a lot of meaning in odd catch-phrases, even grunts and whistles, or we can string together long complicated sentences which actually convey very little, as any politician knows.

In talking with God, every word does have a meaning, but it is a meaning addressed to us. We cannot convey information to Him, "for your Father knows what you need before you ask him." (Matth. 6:8) But He can convey information to us, and the most customary means is through the words that we are using in prayer. They all return to us, informing us, encouraging us, rebuking us, enthralling us. There are many messages, but the substance of them all is the overwhelming love which God has for us, and for each of His holy people.

For example let us take the psalm *De Profundis* (no. 129, or 130 in the Protestant numbering), a favourite prayer when we are conscious of sin, and one that we often use on behalf of those we love who have died. We begin, *Out of the depths I have cried to Thee, O Lord.* God is of course aware that we are calling to Him from the "depths", but maybe He needs to make us aware of it. The "depths" means the immeasurable distance between God as He is, and ourselves, small creatures on a second-class planet. It means the depths of our own inadequacy; the consciousness that we fall far short of being the sort of people that we would like to be, still less the sort of people God plans us to be. In other words it reminds us of sin, the failure to live up to the perfection to which God calls us. It can mean the depths of gloom, of depression, of grief, at the loss of a friend, at the circumstances of our life, at our realisation of how incapable we are of sorting our lives out. It reminds us of how much we need God. And so we continue, *Lord, hear my voice.* There is a strong affirmation, the reassurance that He can and does hear my voice. We do have the possibility of talking with Him, we are not so far down in the depths that we cannot make contact with the Highest. Already we can begin to feel better. We repeat the same idea in different words, *Let Thy ears be attentive to the voice of my supplication.* Yes, of course God the Father does not have ears like ours — but Jesus does. We are reminded that God has become human, that He is one of us after all. He is not alien to our way of thinking, our human physical appearance, for He is a man just like us. It is not inappropriate to talk to God, or about God, using human terms like "ears", since He took the initiative in taking on human life precisely to make it easy for us to communicate with Him, man to man.

But now we come to the important realisation, *If Thou, O Lord, shalt observe iniquities, Lord, who shall endure it?* One of the most important things we need to know is that none of us, neither Mother Teresa nor the Pope, can stand up before God and claim respect in His eyes. God does observe our "iniquities", that is not only the things we do that we would very much rather no one knew about, the things we say that we hope were not heard or at least soon forgotten, but even the thoughts that flit through our minds at the most inappropriate moments. Nothing is concealed from God: and when we realise that, we know that we have nothing to boast about. Anything we have done or said or thought that we might feel pleased about rather pales into insignificance when we remember the sort of things we have been thinking about, the sort of things we might have done and said if the opportunity had been there. Can we endure it? Oh yes, we can, *For with Thee there is merciful forgiveness.* God understands us, He does know how the human mind works, how the human body responds; in fact He knows and understands it far better than we do ourselves. "He knows of what we are made: He understands that are dust." (Psalm 102 (103):14) He is not deceived by our failures nor does He brush them aside as if they do not matter: He actually forgives them. Forgiveness does not mean pretending that everything is all right and brushing aside our apologies with the cold phrase "there's nothing to forgive." There is something to forgive, we really have made a mess of our lives, of the lives of people around us, of the world we were given to live in. God does not make excuses for us, or tell us that we didn't really mean it. He knows full well, and He wants us to know, that our "iniquities" include the deliberate, spiteful, malicious cruelties and betrayals, the sordid thoughts and revolting activities that make up the pattern of our lives. Forgiveness means that all these are wiped out, that the debt has been paid, that we can be and are restored to what we should be, by the one all-sufficient means available, the love of God.

That is less than half the psalm, but enough to illustrate the point that every word is full of meaning, directed towards ourselves. It also illustrates how we can use a familiar "vocal" prayer as the framework for a long discursive meditation. I have by no means exhausted the possibilities of those four lines. We shall come back to this point later, for now it is sufficient to remember the value of words in private prayer.

Now obviously if you stop and think about the meaning of every word like that, and really let it speak to you, it will take at least half an hour to recite any prayer, even the "Our Father". That is an excellent method of prayer, but we do not usually classify it as "vocal" – we have passed the boundary into "mental" prayer. We are told that St Philip Neri taught an uneducated old woman the art of mental prayer by this very means. But not everyone can do this, or at least not every day. "Vocal" prayer is when we recite the words more or less at an ordinary speaking pace.

When we do this, "saying prayers", we cannot possibly be *conscious* of the full meaning of the prayer, but we can and should have the *unconscious intention* of letting every word speak to us. The whole of every possible meaning that we or anyone in the past or future can extract from the text is what we want to express, so that a short prayer can convey an extraordinary amount of meaning in a few words. We need not even go through the entire text: if we remember someone who has died and simply breathe the two words *de Profundis*, that is a single act of the will which intends to reflect on the whole psalm and all it might mean.

It is the same in our ordinary conversations. We use abbreviated or garbled phrases to convey a wealth of meaning, and we understand each other in a much deeper way than the surface sense of the phrase might imply. (This can be very puzzling in a foreign language!) For instance if you see a friend across the street and simply shout "senior!" while waving cheerfully, that means, unpacked, "I hope that in the not too distant future I shall have the pleasure of *seeing you* again, when we shall have more time to talk, but in the meantime I know that you are my friend and you know that I am yours." A lot of meaning can be packed into a very short shout which looks incomprehensible on the page.

That is why it is not inappropriate to repeat set prayers over and over again. If we use, for instance, the Our Father and Hail Mary, many times over, in the course of the Rosary, no one expects us to ponder on the full meaning of every word of the text. What we are doing is making repeated simple acts of the will with the virtual or unconscious intention of expressing all the possible meaning of all the words. In fact, even these acts of the will fuse together into a single act, which is the intention of praying in this particular tradition of the Church.

Vocal Prayer in Common

When we are praying alone, there is no rule that says we have to use such and such a form of prayer, or get through so many prayers each day. The freedom of every individual is to pray in the way that is most helpful to that person that day. We can take the prayers as slowly as we like, and if we do not finish within the time allotted, it does not matter at all.

It is when we are praying with others that we need to be more disciplined. If we are trying to say the Rosary, for instance, along with other people, we must all move more or less at the same pace. However fervent we may feel over the possible sense of the words, to take fifteen minutes over the first half of the first Hail Mary would be very distracting for everyone else. In fact it would be very selfish, imposing our own speed of meditation on others who are expecting to pray more quickly. Meditating out loud is hardly ever helpful for those listening, since we are all different, and what means much to me may mean little to you, while I may be glossing over the very point which you want to spend more time over. No, vocal prayer in common must mean taking the words at an ordinary speaking speed, and keeping pace with each other.

This can be very difficult indeed. In fact many people find it extremely hard to pray aloud with others, whether it be the rosary or any other set prayer. In different places, the prayers are taken at different speeds, so that we are either gasping to catch up or frustrated by long drawn-out meaningful pauses. (The fastest I have ever heard the communal Rosary was in northern Spain, where they can get through it in six minutes; the slowest in Croatia where it takes forty minutes to get through five decades.) We have to remember that for most people it is not actually compulsory to pray aloud in unison with others. All prayer is made in union with the Church, as I have said, but it does not have to be shouted out aloud. Unless we are obliged in some way by a personal commitment, or by the mandate of the Church, the rule in prayer remains still, "as you can and not as you can't".

Liturgical Prayer

The enormous exception is of course in public worship, the liturgy of the Church. That is a vast subject, and not one I ought to attempt to explore here, but it is an obligation on each of us to attend Sunday Mass, and increasingly people want to attend the Divine Office and other functions. But liturgy causes great anxiety, more perhaps than any other aspect of the Faith. Many people admit to being unable to keep their attention on the meaning of the words throughout the Mass, and they feel guilty about that. Those who do not admit to it ought to, for I believe it is not humanly possible to listen to every word of the Mass and be aware of its meaning. The prayers of the Mass are far too long and complicated for that, there are just too many words. We have to use them as shorthand, each prayer no more than a symbol of the wealth of meaning that it conceals, our use of the prayers so many acts of the will, longing and yearning to be united to the love of God.

If we listen attentively to the Introit, the opening verse of Scripture, we may find enough matter for wonder and love to keep us going for a long time. By the time we wake up from thinking about that we may be half way through the second reading. That doesn't matter in the slightest: if at the end of Mass all we remember is the opening two words, we shall have a treasure to carry away. Next time we can hold onto the following two words. In the course of a lifetime we may get all the way through.

Maybe the difficulty is the ordinary form of the Mass as used at present. It was intended and designed to be purely vocal prayer, which means people are liable to feel guilty if they drop into meditation or contemplative prayer. But even in the liturgy the rule still applies, "pray as you can and not as you can't". Mercifully these days the Church permits us a choice, of Mass in the Western or Eastern rite, the ordinary or extraordinary use, said or sung, in Latin or English, in Xhosa, Yoruba or Zulu. We are quite entitled to choose the one we prefer – but we are not entitled to despise those who choose another. During Mass we may try to "follow" the words, or we can put the book down and let the meaning of the Mass flood the soul. We shall want to concentrate on some of the words and remember them – the Gospel for instance – but we cannot possibly concentrate on them all. There will be plenty more to attend to next time we come to Mass.

In a famous passage, Newman describes the Mass as it was celebrated in his time, when the words were understood as "necessary, but as means, not ends, they are not mere addresses to the throne of grace, they are instruments of what is far higher, of consecration, of sacrifice." All who attended Mass prayed "each in his place, with his own heart, with his own wants, with his own thoughts, with his own intention, with his own prayers, separate but concordant, uniting in consummation … like a concert of musical instruments, each different, but concurring in a sweet harmony, we take our part with God's priest, supporting him, yet guided by him. There are little children there, and old men, and simple labourers, and students in seminaries, priests preparing for Mass, priests making their thanksgiving; there are innocent maidens, and there are penitent sinners; but out of these many minds rises one Eucharistic hymn, and the great Action is the measure and the scope of it." (*Loss and Gain*, pp. 327-9) We should be slow to condemn Newman's understanding of the Mass, the one held by so many saints and sinners for nineteen centuries, in favour of the modern "liturgical" view, which might seem so shallow in comparison!

It is the same with the Divine Office. Even though it has been brutally shortened, each part of the Office contains more words than we can hold onto at any one time. We may be content if we can make the prayer our own by a simple act of will, to join our intentions to that of the praying Church. Then we can allow just a verse or two of a psalm to speak to us, while the lips and the surface of the mind run on through all the rest of the text.

Prayer of Repetition

Vocal prayers, all through the history of the Church, have commonly been used in the form of repetition, reciting the same prayer over and over again, whether in groups of three, or ten, fifty or a hundred and fifty. Shorter or longer, repeated prayers have been found helpful in different ways by different people in many traditions.

It is probably still necessary, before going on, to lay the old ghost about "vain repetitions" again. At the back of their minds people are still haunted by the memory that Our Lord might once have said something against using repetition in prayer. The reference is actually to the "King James" (Authorised) version of the Gospel of St Matthew, where the obscure Greek words *mé battologéséte* are translated "use not vain repetitions". This is actually an error, possibly even a deliberate error, introduced as part of a polemic attack on the Catholic use of the Rosary and similar repeated prayers. Whatever the Greek means, it cannot mean anything about repetition. The Revised Standard Version renders it "do not heap up empty phrases", which seems accurate enough – all other modern translations say something similar. It carries on "as the Gentiles do, for they think that they will be heard for their many words. Do not be like them, for your Father knows what you need before you ask Him." (Matt. 6:7-8) In other words, Our Lord is discouraging the use of long complicated verbose prayers, piling up meaningless phrases in the attempt at a high-flown literary composition. As we have already mentioned, such elaborate prayers miss the point of prayer altogether.

There is nothing in the Gospels against repeated prayers, on the contrary they often seem to be highly commended. In the parable of the unjust judge, Our Lord recommends the repeated prayer of those "who cry to him day and night". (Luke 18:7) We think of the blind beggars outside Jericho, calling out over and over, "Have mercy on us, son of David!" (Matt. 20:30) That very prayer, with the addition of the Name of Jesus, forms the most famous of all repeated prayers, the "Jesus Prayer" of the Greek tradition. Many writers from the Eastern church have recommended the use of this prayer, gently repeated in time to the beating of the heart, hence it is also called "Prayer of the Heart". It can be used when sitting still, or walking, lying down or working, on all occasions, so that its most famous exponents recommend it as a means of fulfilling St Paul's command to "pray at all times".

Protestant traditions too, despite their unaccountable devotion to the King James version, make use of often repeated "choruses", short phrases of Scripture sung over and over in a simple rhythmic chant. These can become quite elaborate, as in the "Taizé chants" where the short phrase is repeated as a background to verses sung by a cantor.

In the Catholic church the best-known repetitive prayer is of course the Rosary of St Dominic, with its repeated Hail Marys, originally intended to be the lay-person's equivalent of the Psalter with its 150 Psalms. Another mediaeval favourite was the "Jesus Psalter", also of 150 verses, with a refrain invoking the Name of Jesus, said between every verse. Many other forms of repeated prayer have been used in the West, and it is perhaps a pity that most of them have been forgotten. Among these is

St Philip Neri's short rosary, simply repeating the verse "Holy Mary, Mother of God, pray for us to Jesus", sixty-three times.

When prayer is made in common, a similar practice is the use of a repetitive refrain, like the "Have mercy on us" or "pray for us" in the litanies, or the refrain found in several of the Psalms "for his love endures for ever". The people's part is simply to repeat the refrain, while the priest or other leader makes the invocations. In the Eastern Church, a prayer often repeated is the simple "Lord have mercy", *Kyrie eleison, hospodi pomiluy*, which can be chanted rapidly thirty times in quick succession during Mass, or a hundred and fifty times during one of the Offices.

The purpose of any repeated prayer is not, of course, to reflect on the entire meaning of the words, and to be conscious what God is saying to us through them, again and again and again. To reflect properly on the Hail Mary could take at least half an hour – at that rate there just aren't enough half-hours in the day to get through a daily Rosary. No, what happens when we murmur a prayer over and over again is that we are making simple acts of the will, in an instant unconsciously uniting ourselves to every atom of meaning that we or anyone else could possibly find in those words. It becomes, then, the equivalent of repeated murmurs of love between a mother and child, a lover and his lass. No lover ever thinks that it is enough to express his love for the beloved just once, to state it clearly and efficiently, and then never repeat it again.

If we are truly in love with God, our love will naturally express itself in often-repeated acts of the will, glances towards God; and that is the intention with which we use repeated prayers.

Aspirations

A particular use of a short prayer, often repeated, is what we may call an "aspiration". During the day, especially if it is busy or difficult, we may not have the opportunity for protracted periods of undistracted prayer, but there will be innumerable opportunities for a short one-line prayer, which can, as it were, stitch the day onto heaven. The practice is recommended by one of the great masters of prayer from antiquity, Abba Isaac, who chose the psalm verse "O God, come to my aid, O Lord, make haste to help me!" (Psalm 69 (70):1; see Cassian, *Collations*, Book X, chapter 10.) He points out innumerable possible uses for this verse, in praise, in anxiety, in thanks, in joy. St Benedict recommended it as the way to begin all prayers, which is why it survives to this day as the verse which begins the Divine Office. St Philip Neri (who had also read Cassian) recommended it as a good all-purpose aspiration, as well as other similar verses. Some books collect a number of different texts for use as aspirations, but it is probably better to have just one or two favourites, rather than trying to remember a large selection. Perhaps the most useful are these two: Isaac's psalm verse, "O God, come to my aid, O Lord, make haste to help me!", and the Jesus Prayer, "Jesus, son of the living God, have mercy on me!"

An aspiration has innumerable uses. During work, at any sudden interruption – a telephone or doorbell, an unannounced intruder – a quick prayer will help us to deal with the situation. When driving, at the sudden red light, or the inconsiderate brute swerving in front of us, the dog running into the road, or the traffic unaccountably stationary – an aspiration can be the answer to rising irritation. If we find ourselves muttering unsuitable swear-words (aloud or not), to follow them up with a quick aspiration (not aloud!) means that the most bad-tempered of us will be praying a hundred times a day. If we find our mind wandering onto unsuitable tracks, a quick aspiration will mark our return to our senses. If we are suddenly reminded of some shameful episode in the past, someone long ago that we have hurt or confused, the aspiration can act as a prayer for that person as well as a reminder to ourselves of the present love of God.

Again, when we are at leisure, aspirations can be ideal ways of consecrating our rest and enjoyment to God. When we see the sun setting in red glory, or the moon rising, an aspiration is a good way of giving thanks for the beauties of God's world. When we see someone we love coming towards us, we can sanctify them and our love for them with a short aspiration.

Aspirations have their place during prayer as well. If we wake up to the realisation that our minds have been drifting far away, the aspiration signals our return to our stated intention of prayer. If we find it difficult to keep our place in the book, for the Mass or the Office, the aspiration will cover our fumbling through the pages.

And if we are engaged in trying to write something and find that the words are slow to tumble into place, why then too the aspiration can give meaning to our pause for thought. "O God, come to my aid, O Lord, make haste to help me!"

CHAPTER IV

Thinking about God

There is no stage in anyone's lifetime when we can dare to pretend that we have grown out of vocal prayer, or that the simple prayers we learnt in childhood are no longer necessary. Nevertheless, sooner or later in the life of anyone who prays, they will find themselves drawn into some form of mental prayer, moving from "saying prayers" to "praying".

There are as many different types of mental prayer as there are people who pray, and no one can claim that any particular type is the one and only correct method of prayer. At different stages of life, and on different occasions, we will find different forms of prayer useful; and that can change between morning and evening. But there are certain things which many types of prayer have in common, and these we can perhaps explore together to some extent.

Meditation

To begin with we must waste a little time clearing up some confusion over the word "meditation". Its original use seems to have been for very slow reading, of the type now commonly called *lectio divina*. That means going through a text, either Scripture or the works of one of the saints, and thinking carefully about the meaning of each word. As we shall see, that easily leads into a more silent prayer. At a later stage in Church history the meaning of the word changed, to refer to a more systematic intellectual consideration of the truths of the faith, using texts or "points" as a basis, but with a much more scientific and deliberate approach. Classic books on prayer always use the word in this sense. However in modern times, travellers to India and the Far East observed Hindu or Buddhist holy men engaged in some sort of spiritual exercise, and labelled it with the Catholic word "meditation" without realising how inappropriate this was. As a result most people in the modern world think the word "meditation" means a wordless form of prayer, without conscious thought or imagery, something much more like what classic Christian writers call "contemplation". Nothing can be done about this confusion – all we can do here is to point out that any classic Catholic book on prayer will use the word "meditation" in one way, and most modern authors will use it in quite another. The reader must discern!

Lectio Divina

To return to the older form of "meditation" or mental prayer, let us accept the term *lectio*, since that has become current recently, and is perfectly appropriate. Literally it means "reading", and that is how it starts, though it can certainly be done without carrying a book around. It is taken for granted by the earliest writers on prayer, both in East and West. The works of St John Cassian, written in the early fifth century, display an astonishing insight into human nature, and tell us much about the process of prayer. All later Western writers, at least up to the late sixteenth century, draw on Cassian and his contemporaries, and in one way or other all recommend this slow reflective reading of a sacred text as the principal spiritual activity outside the public liturgy. St Benedict tells each monk to take a book out of the library at the beginning of Lent and use that for his quiet *lectio*, which book might well have lasted him through the year until the next beginning of Lent. (Rule of St Benedict, chapter 48) These authors came from a monastic background, but they were perfectly aware that lay people could and indeed should pray just as much as monks.

It is less natural for us today to read as slowly as that. Reading an ancient book has always been a slow matter, even for those very familiar with the script who use the language as their own. Each sentence must be pondered over, teased out, interpreted. And in the process you have to think what it really means. In the past only the rich could own books, or borrow them from their friends, and even they would have to give up reading small writing as they grew older. That is why short texts were often written up on church walls in very large letters, so that anyone could read them, and ponder on the meaning of the words while using pictures as a visual aid. For instance, on the east wall of many English churches was a painting of Our Lord seated in Judgment, with a scroll saying "Come, ye blessed of my Father". The devout layperson could think about that comforting text, and make it the basis of a mental prayer, perhaps retaining it in his mind as he went about his daily business, and repeating it occasionally while he worked, "Come, ye blessed of my Father". (Or, occasionally, he might need to think about the companion text, "Depart from me, ye accursed". Matth. 25:34, 41) Monks and clerics who had been reading the Psalms in the Divine Office every day since their early teens would know them by heart long before advancing maturity meant they could no longer read for themselves. *Lectio*, therefore, need not always mean actually reading, for it can mean thinking about, ruminating on, a text once read and now committed to memory.

Since the end of the Middle Ages, that sort of slow reading went rather out of fashion, but it has been revived in our own time, and has proved to be a most useful method of prayer for many people. Clear modern print, on smooth modern paper, makes it possible for us to read very quickly. But in the process we may have lost something. When we skim down a page, are we really taking in what we are reading, or is it glancing off the surface of the mind? We may need to learn again how to read slowly, and how to remember. The practice of *lectio*, sitting with an open book in our inner room, or in the church before the Blessed Sacrament, is a good way of helping us to calm down after the rush of daily life.

The technique is to read a few words, a clause or phrase, and then stop, look at the Tabernacle or the Crucifix and be silent. The words may speak to the mind, we may be able to understand their meaning fully. Or they may remain obscure – we go back and read them again, and again until something begins to dawn. Or we may pass on quietly to the next phrase, the next verse, and continue for several lines before realising that we need to go back and start yet again, because a completely different, much more interesting meaning is emerging from the text. If we only read one page in half an hour, that is fine: there is no rush. The Bible will last us a lifetime.

Ruminating on Scripture

If we are reading the Bible, or pondering over a remembered passage, there are several levels on which we can think about it, and the more we practice this sort of meditative reading the more readily we shall discover possible layers of meaning. The literal, historical, meaning of a text may not be the most important. For instance, let us look at Jotham's poem (Judges 9:8-15):

> The trees once went forth to anoint a king over them; and they said to the olive tree, 'Reign over us'. But the olive tree said to them, 'Shall I leave my fatness, by which gods and men are honoured, and go to sway over the trees?' And the trees said to the fig tree, 'Come you, and reign over us'. But the fig tree said to them, 'Shall I leave my sweetness

and my good fruit, and go to sway over the trees?'
And the trees said to the vine, 'Come you, and reign
over us'. But the vine said to them, 'Shall I leave
my wine, which cheers gods and men, and go to
sway over the trees?' Then all the trees said to the
bramble, 'Come you, and reign over us'. And the
bramble said to the trees, 'If in good faith you are
anointing me king over you, then come and take
refuge in my shade; but if not, let fire come out of
the bramble and devour the cedars of Lebanon.'

To start with, the literal meaning is absurd. But it would
be a very stupid person indeed who would say, "Brambles
can't talk, so the whole passage is utter nonsense, and I
won't bother to read it again." We must move at once to
the spiritual sense. There are various different ways of
sub-dividing the spiritual sense, but we can understand
Jotham's poem as an allegory in at least four ways. Firstly
his own intention is clear: you should understand the
bramble to mean Abimelech, the worthless man chosen
to be king when all the best people (represented by the
olive, fig and vine) have declined the post. The ones who
chose him, the men of Shechem, were then horribly
killed by Abimelech. (Judges 9:45-9) That is, I suppose,
the real historical sense of the poem, which we can apply
to our own lives in three ways. We can reflect on the
fact that in almost every country you choose to name,
the worthless men rise to be rulers. The wise and good
decline the post, but all the people suffer from the ones
they themselves have chosen. A second interpretation, in

complete contrast to the former, is to think of Christ in the passage. Now the thorns of the bramble point us in quite the opposite direction: Christ is the lowly one, the despised, the one crowned with thorns, who is the true King because the great ones of this world are too proud to serve – and the fire that comes from Him is the Fire of the Holy Spirit. Thirdly we can apply the passage to ourselves. Are we lowly and despised like the bramble? Are we proud and self-satisfied like the olive and vine? Are we prepared to choose the One crowned with thorns to be our King and let the fire of His love into our hearts?

That is only an outline of the sort of ways we can ponder over a Biblical passage, the sort of reflections we can find in it. It will be genuine prayer if we have the intention of making it prayer, if we want the love of God to speak to us through the text. We may prefer to do it at a desk in a library with dictionaries and concordances to help us, and with pen in hand or keyboard under finger, or we may prefer to do it while walking about, up and down a monastic cloister, or across the hills towards the sea. We may find it surprisingly difficult to do in church in front of the Blessed Sacrament – we shall come to that difficulty later. But in whatever form and whatever place, it is a perfectly valid way of using the text of Scripture in our prayer. (The fourfold exegesis is recommended in the *Catechism of the Catholic Church*, §§115-8.)

It is also the most ancient way, for it is found in Scripture itself. For instance Chapters 3 and 4 of Hebrews are part of a meditation on Psalm 94 (95). Most of the great writers of the first five centuries, the "Church Fathers" wrote in this way, taking a whole book of the Bible and commenting on it line by line, drawing out the spiritual and moral meanings hidden under the literal texts.

The Bible is not, of course, the only book we can use in this way. There are many books by saintly authors which can be treated like this. Any "spiritual reading" can be taken slowly like this, so that we ruminate on the possible meanings of the words, and listen to what God is saying to us through them. That is not to say He cannot speak to us through the words of the telephone directory, but we will probably find it easier to use a "devotional" book in prayerful meditation, and we should remember St Philip's advice to prefer authors with the letters "St" in front of their names.

At the end of this book you will find a list of some spiritual authors that I have found useful over the years.

Pondering Points

A later development in Christian meditation was to approach from entirely the opposite direction, and begin with a point of Catholic doctrine, thinking about that and drawing out its meaning in different ways. This in essence was the "modern devotion" which became popular in the time of Thomas à Kempis and the *Imitation of Christ*, and formalised in the Ignatian method of discursive meditation. In this method, the Bible is quoted or remembered only to confirm our reflections on the doctrinal point. As in the previous method, we always end with our own moral reflections, the application of the point to ourselves, and we should include some reflection on how the point refers to Christ.

For instance, we can take the article in the Creed, "I believe in the Resurrection of the Body." We reflect on what it means: that this human body of mine is to rise again on the last day. If we remember that the Latin text reads *carnis resurrectionem*, the "resurrection of the flesh", we are reminded that we humans are a unity of material and spiritual, we are not all spirit but this too too solid flesh is also caught up into the divine.

When we apply this point to ourselves, we must remember how valuable this material body of ours is. That is why we must look after it, and not despise it. It is true that the early writer Origen believed that in the Resurrection all bodies will be spherical, and certain holy men like St Thomas Aquinas and Blessed John XXIII began to approximate to that shape in this life, but for most of us, keeping it in reasonable shape, without becoming fanatical about health, is also part of our prayer. Moreover precisely because the body is a holy thing, the Temple of the Holy Spirit, destined to rise again, it must be treated with respect – the enemies of the Church can never understand that Catholic sexual morality is based on the belief that the body is good, and indeed sacred.

When we apply the point to Christ, we remember too that the Word was made Flesh, that a human material body is united to the divinity of Christ. And of course it is because of His Resurrection that our own bodies will rise again. The flesh that He gives us is His own Body, in the Eucharist, and it is because we partake in the Eucharist that our bodies become suffused with divinity, and can therefore rise again. A great deal of Catholic doctrine revolves around these few words at the end of the Creed, and there is an enormous amount to ponder on every aspect. Many texts from Scripture, and passages from the saints will occur to us as we revolve around the main point.

That is only an outline of the sort of reflections that can arise when we begin with a doctrinal point. It is the method used in the high and late Middle Ages by the great writers we call the "Scholastics", who worked through Christian doctrine in a systematic way from first principles, illustrating their reflections with quotations from Scripture and the Fathers. But, you will ask, is all this not a description of the study of theology rather than of prayer? That is precisely the point: all valid theology is prayer. Once we detach "theology" from prayer, and turn it into a dry secular academic subject, then it ceases to be valid, and will rapidly degenerate into self-obsessed argument or sceptical infidelity. This is exactly what is wrong with a great deal that passes for theology today. In the great days it was not so. The Fathers of the Church and the great saints of the Middle Ages and Catholic Reformation period did not sit down to write theology for universities – they knelt down to prepare sermons on Scripture for the benefit of their people. In the process they produced great theological insights, but their purpose was prayer, and to help their people to pray.

Use of Imagination

Every faculty of the human person can and should be employed in prayer, and the imagination is no exception. Only, we must remember always that it is our own imagination, not a "vision". When ruminating or meditating on a passage of Scripture we are often recommended to imagine the scene, the characters, their appearance, their words. This is classically called "composition of place". Whether or not we are familiar with the appearance of the Holy Land now, we can all use our imagination to reconstruct what it might have looked like long ago; we all have our imaginary pictures of Our Lord, of the Apostles, the bystanders. We can imagine our own place in the scene, whether we are just bystanders, or taking some part. All this is harmless, and may be very useful in fixing the passage of Scripture in our memory.

In the same way we can imagine a conversation between ourselves and Our Lord, thinking what we would like to say, and what He would be likely to answer. We can even, if the whim takes us, write these things down, or paint great pictures depicting the scene as it has presented itself to our imagination. These may in turn help many others to see the events and appreciate the actions and words of Our Lord. But never for a moment may we forget that it is just our own imagination. Even if we have the artistic skill of Caravaggio, or the poetic skills of Dante, everything we see and hear arises out of our own imagination. It is perilous to start fancying that we are prophets, receiving pictures or words from God!

The images we create, and the words we use to describe them, are ultimately only things that had previously come through the senses, and lie stored in the recesses of the mind, for there is "nothing in the intellect that was not previously in the senses" as St Thomas used to say. However strong the impression made on us, pictures and words we see in prayer are only the reflections of things we have seen, words we have heard. In very exceptional cases God may communicate with us in such a strong way that we actually seem to be hearing words with our ears, seeing scenes with our eyes, but it appears that what happens in these rare cases is that the human mind makes sense of a communication from God by clothing it in the forms we already have to hand. That is why, for instance, even the prophets recognised by the Church have to use the language and dialect of their own people to express what they have heard, the pictures and images at hand to illustrate it. True prophets are rare, false ones multiply in every parish. The false prophet is nearly always someone who has allowed her imagination to run away with her and starts thinking that the pictures she has constructed as "composition of place" are real scenes, the words she has put into the mouth of Our Lord or Our Lady are real messages from heaven. It is usually pretty obvious that these "messages from heaven" are illusionary, pious platitudes, or flattery of the self-styled prophet. Occasionally they are really dangerous, like the prophecy that told the Xhosa people to kill all their cattle and burn their granaries. The Church is usually quick to spot the false prophet, but not always quite quick enough. (A good guide to discernment of prophecy is Fr Benedict Groeschel's *A Still Small Voice*, Ignatius 1993.)

If we avoid that danger, as I said, there is no harm at all in using the imagination, and even being aware that God can speak to us through it. The message will still be the same one, of His love for us, and His commandment to love one another. And it will be a message for us alone. We must never start fancying that we are in any way special, chosen to tell other people things they don't already know. To know the love of God, and to put it into practice is a full-time occupation for any of us.

CHAPTER V

Lord, Teach us to Pray

As an illustration of much that has come before, let us take the most fundamental of all prayers and examine how God speaks to us through it. We will follow the text as we know it by heart, in St Matthew's Gospel (Matth. 6:9-13), but keeping a finger in the place where St Luke reports it slightly differently (Luke 11:1-4). Many saints and holy men have written meditations on the Our Father, and all are worth reading, but it can never be exhausted. Prayer has been described as drinking from a fountain: no matter how often we come back, there is still more flowing out to greet us.

The disciples asked Our Lord to teach them to pray, "just as John taught his disciples". In passing, it would be fascinating to know exactly how John the Baptist taught them, and why the disciples, many of whom had been disciples of John beforehand, knew that was not enough. Our Lord does not give them a "method" or "technique", and it is unlikely John the Baptist did either. He says nothing about posture or breathing, about times and numbers. He introduces it with the advice not to pile up bombastic phrases like the pagans, "for your Father knows what you need before you ask Him." (Matth. 6:8) That does not rule out prayer of petition, as we have said, but it does rule out the idea that we somehow have to instruct God. "It is one thing to inform someone who is ignorant, quite another to make a request of one who knows us well", as St Jerome said. (Our quotations in this chapter from St Jerome and the other Church Fathers come from the *Catena Aurea* of St Thomas Aquinas, a commentary on the Gospel made up of passages from all the great writers, as if they were sitting around a table discussing it verse by verse. An English translation was prepared by Newman and his friends at Littlemore, and reprinted in 1997.)

Prayer is not an exercise in elegant prose composition to persuade an unwilling God to give us what we want. St Augustine said, "there should not be much speaking, just much prayer." We cannot impress Him by our diligence, our perseverance, our squeezed-out emotions, any more than we can by our posture or phraseology. Nor should we pray for the sake of the effect on other people, even if we fancy we are setting them a good example, let alone if we imagine they will be impressed by our overweening goodness. That is why Our Lord says we should pray "in secret, and your Father who sees in secret will reward you." (Matth. 6:6)

The Our Father contains within itself all the prayers of the Old and New Testament, and includes everything that it could possibly be right for us to pray. For that reason all other prayers are, in a way, no more than expansions of the Our Father, and any prayer that contradicts the Our Father is invalid. For the Our Father is, above all, the Lord's Prayer – meaning by that the prayer He makes Himself, as well as the one He gives to us.

Why are there two versions? Without getting entangled in the fruitless task of looking for the "sources of the Gospels", we may note that St Matthew and St Luke describe two different occasions, and we need not be surprised if Our Lord chose to vary the actual words He used. Moreover He probably gave them the words in Aramaic, and what we have is only two English translations of two different Greek translations. In essence, the two versions are the same: a few phrases are omitted in St Luke, but the sense is included in those which remain. We may note in passing that the very differences prove the authenticity of the text. As so often in the Gospels, we have two independent witnesses, who record for us effectively the same words, although they were spoken on different occasions.

The Ten Commandments come to us in two different versions in exactly the same way (Exod. 20 and Deut. 5). This may be taken as a prophecy of the fact that the Our Father reflects the structure of the Ten Commandments, speaking first of God, secondly of our neighbour. There are three Commandments about our love of God, and there are three petitions in the Our Father that call us to "love the Lord our God with all our heart and with all our soul and with all our might." There are seven Commandments about our neighbour, and four petitions in the Our Father which mean, in effect, "love thy neighbour as thyself". In this way the whole of the Old Testament law is summed up and fulfilled in the Lord's Prayer.

Our Father

And so we begin by calling God "our Father". It is characteristic of Our Lord to call God His Father, and in many places in the Gospels we hear Him doing so. Many times He prays directly, *Pater*, "Father!", and St Mark records the Aramaic word *Abba!* (Mark 14:36) St Paul later on tells us to do the same: "God has sent the Spirit of his Son into our hearts, crying, 'Abba, Father!'" (Gal. 4:6; cf. Rom. 8:15)

This is something radically new in the religion of Israel. It is extremely rare to find anyone in the Old Testament call God "Father". To be precise, it is only once each in the two very late books, the Wisdom of Solomon and the Wisdom of ben Sirach, that we find that form of address for God (Wisd. 14:3; Sir. 23:4). In all the older books, God is called "the Most High", the "Almighty", the "Lord", "my God" (Psalm 90 (91):1-2), and frequently "God of our fathers" or "God of my father David" and the like; many other forms of address are invoked, but never "Father", still less *Abba*. But there are prophets who look forward to the time when someone will appear who will call Him "Father". "He shall cry to me, 'Thou art my Father, my God, and the Rock of my salvation'" (Psalm 88 (89):26). "Have you not just now called to me, 'My Father, thou art the friend of my youth'? ... I thought you would call me 'My Father', and would not turn from following me." (Jeremiah 3:4, 19) Moreover, one prophet looks forward to the time when many others will call God "Father", even though they are not Israelites: "For thou art our Father, though Abraham does not know us and Israel does not acknowledge us; thou, O LORD, art our Father, our Redeemer from of old is thy name." (Isaiah 63:16)

These prophecies are fulfilled in the life of Our Lord, and in our own lives. Throughout his life on earth Jesus calls God "my Father", beginning when He was twelve years old. "Did you not know that I must be in my Father's house?" (Luke 2:49) Moreover when addressing his disciples, He frequently refers to God as "your Father", particularly in St Matthew's Gospel. "It is not you who speak, but the Spirit of your Father speaking through you." (Matth. 10:20) Above all, it is in St John's Gospel that we hear Our Lord calling God His Father, and inviting us to do the same. We become children of God by growing into unity with His Son, Jesus. There are those who refuse to accept this, "Abraham is our father!" say the Pharisees. And there are those who are slow to understand. Philip foolishly asks Jesus to "show us the Father", and Our Lord rebukes him, "He who has seen me has seen the Father; how can you say, 'Show us the Father'?" (John 14:9) At the very end He tells them, "I am ascending to my Father and your Father, to my God and your God." (John 20:17) We too are now entitled to call God by the same name with which Christ addressed Him, for we are also children of God. The life we have, as children of the Father, is the life of the Holy Spirit, the gift of the Father and the Son, who breathes in us, and who alone can teach us to pray. In saying *"Our* Father" we affirm our unity, the fact that we never pray alone. We pray always as one of a family. The existence of the Church depends on recognition of that common paternity, as St Paul writes "to the church of the Thessalonians in God our Father, and the Lord Jesus Christ". (I Thess. 1:1)

... *who art in heaven* ...

Many times, too, Our Lord refers to our Father as being in heaven, "that you may be sons of your Father who is in heaven". (Matth. 5:45, cf. Matth. 11:25) We must not imagine that people in Our Lord's time were so naive as to imagine that heaven is a place, one that could be reached by climbing a mountain or flying into the sky, any more than they believed hell was to be found by digging. Oh yes, they used "up" and "down" as metaphors, and we do exactly the same now; in most languages the words for heaven and "sky" are the same. But they knew there was more to it than that. "Behold heaven and the highest heavens cannot contain thee", prayed Solomon (I Kings 8:27), well aware that the presence of God transcends anything we can imagine in space or time. The Heavens, as the Old Testament prefers to express it, means the whole realm of invisible creation, which is not spatially removed from us, but interpenetrates the visible world. Heaven is not far away: God is all around us, indeed the "Kingdom of God is among us". (Luke 17:21) Nor is heaven immaterial, we must not project Greek philosophical ideas of "matter" and "spirit" into the scriptures. The heavenly bodies are solid enough in their own sphere, which is why Moses speaks of a "firmament", a solid base (Gen. 1:6). When we speak of the resurrection of the body, we are affirming the reality and solidity of heaven. In heaven exists the risen body of Our Lord, the assumed body of Our Lady; there too is our own destiny if we accept a share in the Resurrection.

When we call on our Father in heaven, on one level our prayer simply makes a distinction between Him and our fathers on earth, on another level we affirm our union with the Father through our union with the Son. Earthly fathers are only called so by analogy with our heavenly Father; they are usually a disappointment, failing utterly to live up to the model presented to them. Yet everything in them that is "fatherly" is derived from the true Fatherhood of God the Creator, the "Father, from whom every family in heaven and on earth is named." (Eph. 3:14) That is why we are "to call no man your father on earth", for only God is really Father (Matth. 23:9). In that passage Our Lord is certainly not telling us to refuse to "honour our father and our mother": he is clear that this commandment stands, and must be observed (Matth. 15:4, 19:19). No, here he is warning us against treating our earthly fathers as being truly the ones responsible for our existence, whether we call them fathers because of their physical parenthood, or out of courtesy for a spiritual paternity such as St Paul loved to claim. "I became your father", he writes, "in Christ Jesus through the gospel". (I Cor. 4:15) Our Lord warns our physical fathers against the sort of high-handed domination of their children that was the custom among the pagans, whereby a father could ruin the lives of his children even to the extent of claiming the right of life and death over them. Only God, our true Father, has the right to our absolute obedience; only He has the true power of life and death. That is why "a man shall leave father and mother" (Matth. 19:5), and "he is not worthy of me who loves father or mother more". (Matth. 10:37) In the same way spiritual fathers must guard against claiming overweening authority over those in their care, and setting themselves up as "masters" when we have, in truth, only one Master, the Christ (Matth. 23:10).

All that is important, but far more important is our affirmation that we are all the children of the one Eternal Father, that we know ourselves to be so because of our Eucharistic union with Jesus his Son, that we are brothers and sisters of each other. We affirm that we are able to call on the Father, directly, with no intermediary, and we are confident that He hears us. "Father, I thank thee that thou hast heard me. I knew that thou hearest me always." (John 11:41-2)

... hallowed be thy name.

We pray that His Name will be made holy – in effect that "it will be made holy in us" (St John Chrysostom). We are to be the agents of that sanctification, we, His children, are to diffuse that holiness throughout the world. We are praying that God will bring about a change in us, so that when people see us they will "give glory to our Father who is in heaven." (Matth. 5:16)

"Holiness" and "Glory" are both aspects of the same thing, the characteristic of belonging to God. In the Old Testament "holiness" was thought of as a quality that could be conferred by God onto His chosen people, onto their land, the Holy Land, to the Temple built to the glory of his name, and onto the objects necessary for worship in that Temple. Holiness could be transferred by contact from one object to another: it was infectious, contagious, almost like radioactivity. Anything marked as "Holy" could not be put to a profane use: "an outsider shall not eat of a holy thing" (Lev. 22:10); anyone who makes holy incense privately "to use as perfume shall be cut off from his people" (Exod. 30:38); to use the holy vessels from the Temple as ordinary drinking cups brought about the destruction of Babylon (Daniel 5); to invade the Temple itself invited severe retribution (II Maccabees 3); to invade the Holy Land was to challenge the supremacy of God Himself (II Kings 18:32-5). Thus to be "sanctified", "made holy" or "hallowed" means to belong to God: we must accept our intrinsic holiness as children of God, and do all we can to extend awareness of holiness to those we meet. Holiness in itself does not mean the same thing as virtuous, but we cannot say this prayer sincerely unless we want holiness to translate itself in our lives as personal goodness, nor can we hope to bring others to understand the love of God unless we make some attempt to respond to God's call to virtue and goodness.

"Glory" in the Scriptures means the manifestation of the presence of God, the unbearable light which surrounds His throne. Glimpses of it were granted to Moses, though mercifully veiled under the Cloud of Unknowing (Exod. 19:16-19; 34:5, 29), and to Solomon in the newly dedicated Temple (I Kings 8:10-11). St John himself had seen something of the Glory, when he and James and Peter had witnessed the Transfiguration of Jesus. "We have beheld his glory, glory as of the only Son from the Father." (John 1:14)

The Name, in Scripture, means very much more than a mere proper noun. "Why do you ask My Name, seeing it is wonderful?" (Judges 13:18) Moses asked the Lord to tell him His Name, and there was revealed to him the Name which may not be spoken, YHWH, the One who Is and Was and Will Be (Exod. 3:14). It is God's very nature to exist; He is the source of all existence. In revealing that Name, God both grants Moses' request and refuses it. He reveals the truth about who He is, but He refuses to take on himself a name like any other name, as if He were just one more in a long list of gods and goddesses who might be useful to Moses. That is why it is so wrong to attempt to write vowels into the Name and to pronounce it, as the Pope has clearly told us. "The Israelites were perfectly right in refusing to utter this self-designation of God, expressed in the word YHWH, so as to avoid degrading it to the level of names of pagan deities. By the same token, recent Bible translations were wrong to write out this name – which Israel always regarded as mysterious and unutterable – as if it were just any old name." (Benedict XVI, *Jesus of Nazareth*, p. 143)

Writing out that Name is something that causes scandal and offence to the Jews, but never more so than when that Name was written up over the body of an executed criminal. By one of the most bizarre workings of Providence, a Jewish hand wrote this, at the dictation of a pagan:

Yehoshua HaNozri, WuMelek HaYehudim

Jesus the Nazarene, and King of the Jews.

Pilate surely did not know or realise what prophecy he was uttering, though he claimed responsibility for it: "what I have written, I have written." (John 19:19, 22) The Name that was so publicly disgraced has become the "Name above all other Names". (Phil. 2:9) That is why we are to keep it holy.

The second Commandment is "You shall not take the Name of the LORD your God in vain." (Deut. 5:11) That means very much more than a prohibition on casual swearing, important too though that is. It means that in all we do and say and think we must be aware of the love of God within us, and we should convey that love to all around us. If we obscure the love of God by our words or actions, we are preventing His Name from being held holy, keeping others from seeing the face of God. For those outside will always judge the Church by us, those who do not know God can only come to know Him by observing us.

Our Lord's own prayer includes the hallowing of the Name. "Now is my soul troubled, and what shall I say? 'Father, save me from this hour'? No, for this purpose I have come to this hour. Father, glorify thy name." (John 12:27-8) Then a little later, after Judas had gone out and night had fallen, Jesus said, "Now is the Son of man glorified, and in him God is glorified." (John 13:31) The glorification of the Name of God is the suffering and death of Christ. That is the great paradox that underlies the whole of St John's Gospel, that the Cross is the moment of triumph and of glory. The Name that is to be glorified is the one scratched on the board above the Cross. It is in the mocking and scorning of the Name that it is made most glorious. He conquers by accepting defeat.

All this is expanded in the great Prayer of Christ after the Last Supper (John 17). In this prayer, indeed, the whole of the Our Father is included, and we can see how Our Lord teaches us to pray exactly as He prays. "Father, the hour has come: glorify thy Son that the Son may glorify thee ... and now, Father, glorify thou me in thy own presence with the glory which I had with thee before the world was made. I have manifested thy name." (John 17:1, 5, 6)

Our Lord said, "Blessed are the pure in heart, for they shall see God." (Matth. 5:8) As in all the Beatitudes, we have here a note of the character of Jesus Himself, the one whose heart is pure, who constantly sees the Father. He alone fulfils perfectly the command to "love the LORD your God with all your heart." (Deut 6:5) The sight of God is more than human kind can bear — in the Old

Testament those who saw no more than an angel were terrified, "We shall surely die, for we have seen God." (Judges 13:22) Moses himself could not bear to look directly at God, he saw Him only veiled in the Cloud, or concealed in the cleft of the rock. To look directly at God is impossible for us, we can see Him only in shadows and images, under symbols and veils.

It is only in the heart, the innermost part of our being, that we can see God, and yet he who has seen Jesus has seen the Father (John 14:9). We see God in the human form of His Son, the Word made flesh. "We have seen with our eyes, we have looked upon and touched with our hands ..." (I John 1:1) Because God has shown himself to us in human form, we need no longer dread seeing Him as he really is: "when he appears we shall be like Him, for we shall see Him as He is." (I John 3:2) That is, if we are pure of heart. "Who shall ascend the hill of the LORD? He who has clean hands and a pure heart." (Psalm 23 (24):3-4) To see God we must avert our gaze from anything less than God, direct ourselves whole-heartedly towards Him. To be "pure of heart" means very much more than being continent and chaste, though that is certainly part of it: it means not allowing ourselves to be dragged away from our love for the Father by "the lust of the flesh and the lust of the eyes and the pride of life". (I John 2:16) No, none of us can claim to be pure of heart, "if we say we have no sin we deceive ourselves" (I John 1:8), but we can be totally confident of God's forgiveness if we once have the courage to admit that we need it. Never can we be satisfied with anything less than purity of heart, but at the same time if we acknowledge that we are not yet pure in heart, then "he will forgive our sins and cleanse us from all unrighteousness". (I John 1:9)

It will take us a long time to be cleansed from sin, at least one lifetime, and at the end of our lives most of us will still not be clean in His eyes, but we can trust in His love to cleanse us, and purify us, in this life and after it, so that eventually, truly pure of heart, we shall be able to see God, to glorify His name, and His Name will be hallowed in us.

Thy kingdom come ...

The concept of "kingdom" may seem to be unfamiliar or strange – indeed the superficial may think it is out of date, since kings and kingdoms have become rare on the earth. The truth is exactly the opposite: the disappearance of kings from our daily life means that the Kingdom of God need no longer be obscured by our experience of unsatisfactory earthly kingdoms.

Just as the word "Father" is properly used only of God, and is transferred by analogy to biological or spiritual fathers, most of whom fall very far short of the model, in the same way the word "Kingdom" is properly used only of the Kingdom of Heaven. It means that God has a supreme and unchallenged authority, that His loving will is the force that governs and directs the entire creation, and that our response to Him must be one of loving acceptance and joyous conformity. Only He can truly "reign", only He truly deserves allegiance. In several of the Psalms we acclaim the LORD as our only true King (e.g. Psalms 92 (93), 96 (97), and 98 (99) all begin "The LORD is king", or "The LORD reigns").

That is why when the Israelites first demanded to have a king just like all the nations around them, the prophet was indignant. "And the LORD said to Samuel, 'Hearken to the voice of the people in all that they say to you; for they have not rejected you, but they have rejected me from being king over them.'" Samuel warned the people exactly why having a king would be a bad idea, but they refused to listen to him. "And in that day you will cry out because of your king whom you have chosen for yourselves; but the LORD will not answer you in that day." (I Sam. 8:4-22) They had already suffered from the self-imposed rule of "King" Abimelech (Judges 9), they were to suffer a great deal more from the succession of Kings of Israel and Judah whose disreputable stories occupy such a large part of the historical books of the Old Testament. By the time of Our Lord they had to cope with the appalling maladministration of the Herod family, not to mention the decadent tyranny of the Roman Emperors (who were known as "kings" in the East). The miracle of Our Lord's legal descent as recounted by St Matthew (1:1-17) is that from such an unsatisfactory line of squalid or weak monarchs came the Christ, the one real King who was to rule all the nations.

When the institution of monarchy seemed to be vanishing from the earth, Pope Pius XI instituted the devotion and feast of Christ the King. Christ is the true King who can summon our allegiance, the only real monarch of our hearts. At a time when totalitarian republics were tyrannising over God's people, and the blood of martyrs flowed in a deeper stream than ever before, the champions of Christ called out "Long live Christ the King!" to proclaim their true loyalty, their deepest allegiance. For, as Our Lord prayed, "They are not of the world, even as I am not of the world. Sanctify them in the truth; thy word is truth. As thou didst send me into the world, so I have sent them into the world." (John 17:16-18)

This is not, of course, to say, that there may not be such a thing as Christian monarchy on earth, just as there are Christian fathers on earth. But it does affirm that our allegiance to Her Gracious Majesty is provisional, and that we will obey her and her government only when they are in accordance with God's law. In the case of the first Queen Elizabeth, who demanded subservience beyond that given to God, the saints had to refuse, and the result was hundreds of martyrdoms. A modern monarch reigns but does not rule and it is the "elected" government of the day that commands our allegiance, rather than the person of the monarch, but the principle is exactly the same. We should obey the government in all things neutral, all things beneficial and in accordance with the rule of God, but if a government, however democratic, tries to make us disobey the Kingdom of God, then we must resist. "We must obey God rather than men" (Acts 5:29). Modern republican governments can be even more tyrannical and intolerant than Tudor monarchs, and martyrdom for the Kingdom of Heaven is by no means a thing of the past. King Solomon prayed for "an understanding mind to govern thy people" (I Kings 3:9), but many modern rulers have no such good intentions.

The third Commandment, "Observe the sabbath day, to keep it holy" (Deut. 5:12), is a reminder that all time belongs to God, and that all our work may only be done for Him and through Him. If we consecrate the week by setting aside one day in seven for prayer and rest, for families together, then there will be a blessing on all that we do. Modern governments, driven by the relentless worship of commerce, have effectively abolished the sabbath. We can hardly complain if no blessings descend on our work. Yet even now, if we observe the sabbath, keeping Sunday as a day for God, we will find that our weekly work is more efficient, even if only through the natural effect of taking time to rest. In modern conditions of employment, preserving Sundays for God and for our families may involve almost heroic resistence, a weekly challenge to put Christ the King first in our lives.

When we call on God, saying, "Thy Kingdom come", we are calling on Him to bring about that Kingdom in our lives. We are the heirs of that Kingdom – but where is it to be found? Our Lord tells us, "The Kingdom of God is within you" or "among you" (Luke 17:21), and there has been much debate about what He meant. In truth, all the possible meanings of that phrase are correct. The Kingdom is "within" us, because it is our own hearts that have to be the throne of Christ, our own bodies to be temples of the Holy Spirit. He Himself *is* the Kingdom, as the Holy Father has explained (*Jesus of Nazareth*, pp. 49, 60-61). Unless Jesus rules within us, unless we accept Him into ourselves and welcome His rule in heart and mind and strength, His rule cannot extend outside us. For His rule is the rule of love, the love of God which must be planted in our hearts so that it can blossom in our lives, and extend to those around us. That love can be terribly strong, "love is as strong as death… many waters cannot quench love". (Song 8:6, 7) The love of God may involve great effort, heroic sacrifice, determination, and courage, so that we can "love the LORD our God with all our might". (Deut 6:5)

But the Kingdom is also "among you". Our Lord was speaking to the Pharisees, who were unaware that the reign of God on earth had already begun. Unknown to them, a little flock of fishermen and tax-collectors, women and children from the poorer classes, was already the nucleus of a Kingdom which was to extend throughout the world. "The Kingdom of God", said Our Lord, "is like a mustard seed". It is small, and unattractive; left to itself it will grow into a mustard plant, maybe a few centimetres high to be eaten in sandwiches with cress, or perhaps growing to its full height of thirty centimeters or so and producing spicy seeds for a relish – nothing very spectacular. But in this case the mustard seed is going to grow, "till it becomes a tree, and the birds of the air will come and nest in its branches." (Matth. 13:31-2, cf. Daniel 4:10-12) Beyond all expectation, far beyond the possibilities of natural growth, the supernatural growth of the Kingdom of Heaven has seen that frightened group of Galileans become a Church well over a billion strong.

And again the Kingdom of God is "among you". Our Lord uses another parable: it is like the yeast "which a woman took and hid in three measures of flour, till it was all leavened." (Matth. 13:33) The yeast ceases to be visible when it is kneaded into the dough; the Kingdom ceases to be visible when it is diffused through all mankind. This parable has been fulfilled in our own lifetime, as the movements of peoples across the world have brought it about that the Church is now dispersed and scattered through every nation on earth, as never before. There was a time when all the Catholics in the world were concentrated in a very few lands – now we are everywhere, though in less concentration. It is tempting to look back with longing at the High Middle Ages, when almost every living soul in Europe was Catholic, and the great spiritual writers were filling Europe with their teaching. But in those days there was not a single Christian anywhere in Africa south of the Sahara, any more than in Australia or the Americas. What proportion of the human race was Christian then? Probably less than now. And of those who believed themselves to be Christian what proportion were truly holy, subjects of the Kingdom? To judge by what those great spiritual writers say about their contemporaries, not very many. In Christian Europe there were very many men and women who gave themselves over to lives of greed, lust or anger even though they attended Mass every Sunday. In our own time, the Church, kneaded into the lump of humanity, contains a greater proportion of the human race than ever before; and from the very fact of our dispersal among the hostile nations, probably contains a higher proportion of men and women who are genuinely trying to conform themselves to the Kingdom of God, and let the love of God radiate out through them. The prayer, "Thy Kingdom come", uttered so often by so many millions, looks as if it is being granted well enough in our days.

As always, when there are several possible interpretations of a phrase of Scripture, the most Catholic answer is to accept them all. There is yet another meaning of the Kingdom of God – the final consummation of all things at the end of history. For a while in the late twentieth century that became something of an obsession in the Church, and is given an extraordinary prominence even in authoritative late twentieth-century texts. All too easily, it could be used as an excuse for neglecting charity in this world. This could have been a reaction to the obsession of the previous generations, which was to reduce the Kingdom to purely earthly terms, eliminating both Christ and His Church in order to concentrate on building a new social order. (See the incisive criticism of this-worldly Kingdom making, and the fundamental error of Karl Marx, in Benedict XVI, *Spe Salvi*, §§ 16-21.) In contrast, the obsession with the End of the World eliminated any social aspect to the Gospel, on the lines of, "everything is about to come to an end, so there is no point in wasting time feeding the poor, clothing the naked, welcoming the stranger and so on." No point? But did not Our Lord tell us that we shall be judged precisely on how we have carried out those works of charity? (Matth. 25:31-46) If the world comes to an end while we are in the middle of building a hospital, constructing an education system, teaching the poor how to fish – in what better state could we be found? Yes, the final bringing in of the Kingdom will mean the end of history, the end of our human activity in this world, but it will not mean the end of charity. The End will be a great and glorious day, but it is not at all clear that we should pray for it to come soon – in fact, as we shall see, it may be that we are really meant to pray for its delay. We are certainly commanded not to fret about it, still less to waste time trying to calculate the date. Each of us individually will come to judgment soon enough, and we pray that the Kingdom will come in our lives then as now, but we should continue to build up the church and to work for charity in the state for the benefit of many generations to come.

Our Lord said, "Blessed are the poor in spirit, for theirs is the kingdom of heaven." (Matth. 5:3) The Kingdom is promised to the poor, the poor in spirit. In St Luke's version (Luke 6:20) it is more simply, "Blessed are you poor, for yours is the kingdom of God." Yet that does not exclude the "poor in spirit", for St Luke's gospel shows us clearly how we must come before God with empty hands for Him to fill them. The poor are those who are despised and overlooked in this world: never before had anyone called their position "blessed" or even "joyous" (the Greek word can mean both). Power, the kingdom of this world, seems to lie exclusively in the hands of the rich, or at least those who have set their sights on being rich. God's kingdom is offered to those who are poor.

The experience of the destruction of Jerusalem and the Exile had shown God's people that rewards do not come in this life: it is better to be materially poor but faithful. They were content to be the "poor of the LORD", as long as they were confident of their virtue before God (Sirach 35:17). What is new in the Gospel is the realisation that we cannot even claim our own virtue: we come before God with nothing, "He has regarded the low estate of his handmaiden... He who is mighty has done great things for me." (Luke 1:48-9) Our Lord commends the prayer of the publican who has nothing whatsoever to offer God; ill gotten wealth, maybe, but he knows that he has neither virtue nor integrity, "God, be merciful to me, a sinner." (Luke 18:13) The distinction "poor in spirit" firstly means those who are willingly poor, those who embrace the freedom that comes from not being encumbered with the responsibility of material wealth. It is obviously possible to be materially poor and at the same time greedy, grasping, obsessed with keeping hold of the little we have and determined to make ourselves rich one day. To be "poor in spirit" must mean to be happy with what little we have, to be generous in sharing it, to have no great ambitions except to spread the love of God around us. Secondly it means accepting that we are spiritually poor, that we can make no claim against God, that we come to him with nothing to boast about in our morals, our devotion, even our faith. Only when we know that we are empty can God fill us.

"The saints are the true interpreters of Holy Scripture", as the Pope tells us (*Jesus of Nazareth*, p. 78).

The chronicles of the saints are full of stories of the "poor in spirit". Some began by being exceedingly rich in the world's terms, and using their wealth and position effectively in practical works of charity, so that the love of God radiated out from them into the lives of many. Such were people like St Elizabeth of Hungary, or her namesake of Portugal. They did great works with great riches, and died in poverty in possession of the Kingdom of Heaven. Others were never distinguished in the eyes of the world but went about quietly giving what they could, using small incomes to spread great love. Such were St Philip Neri and his companions, who never renounced the possession of their small means, but used them to great effect. And others there were who undertook the voluntary renunciation of all property, gave up everything in this world, and lived solely for the love of God. Such were St Antony of Egypt, and Blessed Charles de Foucauld. The greatest of the saints were those who knew that they came before God with empty hands, holding them open to Him, like Thérèse of Lisieux. Of all these is the Kingdom of Heaven; only through this sort of poverty of spirit can the Church be reformed.

Thy will be done ...

We call on God to bring about what He wills. At first that might seem strange – why should we make a point of asking Him to do what He Himself wishes to do? Of course what we are asking for is the ability to carry out His will in our own lives, that He may mould us, conform us to

His will, so that we ourselves willingly do what He wills. In other words we are praying for the grace to be docile and obedient. That the will of the Father should be carried out in us may seem to be little more than a repetition of the idea of the coming of the Kingdom, which is presumably why this petition is omitted in St Luke's version (Luke 11:2). But there is so much more in it. The will of God includes every aspect of creation, from the smallest microbe to the greatest stars, but the culmination of His creation is man, and it is in our own lives that His will must triumph.

It is remarkably difficult to be docile and obedient. However much we may think we desire to obey the will of God, we find over and over again that we have failed to do it. "I do not do the good I want, but the evil I do not want is what I do ... . For I delight in the law of God, in my inmost self, but I see in my members another law at war with the law of my mind and making me captive to the law of sin which dwells in my members." (Rom. 7:19, 22-3) Can any of us claim that these words of St Paul do not apply to ourselves? We know perfectly well what would be the right and good thing to do, but we persist in doing the opposite. And it happens over and over again. It is the common experience of humankind, that we are not fully in control of our own thoughts, words, actions and omissions. Every human creature has, as Newman teaches us, by nature a conscience (*Grammar of Assent*, p. 105): all of us are capable of knowing God's will for our lives. But all of us fail in the attempt to carry it out.

What a comfort it is to know that the greatest saints have felt the same way, and recorded their feelings for us. Not St Paul alone, but every saint who has left any written record of that struggle towards love tells us the same thing. Look at the *Imitation of Christ* (Book III, ch. 50), for the same message, expanded but essentially exactly what St Paul said. If the heroes of our faith were aware of the struggle between good and evil in their lives, aware of their frequent failures and mistakes, and the need to rise above them again and again, we need not be discouraged in our own struggle to be good. We do have persistent weaknesses, and those weaknesses can be so strong that they drag us away from what we really want to do, prevent us from being the sort of people we really want to be.

That is not to say that we are totally out of control. We are not helpless puppets, dashed around by hormones and stress. We are partially free, imperfectly human. The only perfect humans are Our Lady and her Son – the rest of us are all damaged in one way or another. There is, in all of us, a good side that really does desire the will of God, and in all of us there is the opposite. Our life is played out between these two opposing forces. As long as we continue to struggle, victory is certain, for we have been redeemed and sanctified by Christ, but the war is not yet over. We pray every day "thy will be done", because we know that every day we need to be reminded of the need to want to do God's will. We are aware of two forces struggling within us, the will to good, the tendency to evil. As long as the will to good keeps up the struggle, we are winning, for if God is on our side, who can be against us? (cf. Rom. 8:31) This is what it means to "love the LORD your God with all your soul" (Deut. 6:5), the soul that is our true inmost being longing to do His will.

Without the help of God we cannot do His will; left to ourselves we would decay into total corruption very quickly indeed. That is why we need that help from God which we call Grace, continually, today and every day. It is Grace that makes us want to love God, it is Grace that makes us want to love our neighbour. It is Grace that makes it possible for us to resist the forces of laziness and inertia and selfishness which do so much to hold us back. Grace is an aspect of the love of God: it is the dynamism which He gives us in order that we may be able to listen to His voice, able to rise above our mistakes and faults and malicious sins, able to carry out in our lives whatever He wills to be the best for us, and to be the best for those around us.

Grace cannot operate in us unless we consent – that is the greatest mystery of God's love for us. He does not force us to do His will. Love is not love if it is forced. Love must be free, and so we are free to "receive with meekness the implanted word" of God. (James 1:21) Or we are free to reject it. The First Commandment is, "you shall have no other gods before me." (Deut. 5:7) If we place anything at all before the Will of God we are in effect worshipping false gods, setting up little idols which challenge our Creator in His own world, in our lives, in the lives of those around us. We are free to reject God's Will, yes, but what good can come of that? The idols, the false gods, will always disappoint us. Only God is true, only the true God is loving, only the love of God will bring us happiness. But we are free to destroy our own happiness and that of others by rejecting the loving Will of God.

There is a real mystery – how can we frustrate the will of God? He is all powerful, yes, He can do whatever He wants, yes. But He chooses not to force the issue: He chooses to hold back His power and suspend His own will, He makes Himself dependent entirely on the feeble weak-willed stubborn idiotic resistance which the least of us puts up to His will.

When we resist His will, when we refuse to do what He desires for us, that is what we call Sin. And sin has consequences not only in our own lives but in the lives of other people around us. Sin can cause terrible suffering; any disruption of the Will of God for His creation is bound to cause unhappiness. Moreover the suffering may not always be our own, or that of people close to us – our sins can cause appalling suffering for people we have never met, whose lives are far distant from us in space or time. Yet God binds Himself to let this happen, rather than deny the very nature of love by interfering and preventing us from sin.

That is why we talk of God's will as "permitting" terrible things to happen – not that they are directly willed by Him, far from it, but that they happen as a result of the free choice made by free agents to resist and contradict His will. Abbot Chapman makes it clear in one of his *Spiritual Letters* (no. LXXXIII, p. 233), "God's Will towards us is:– (1). *Voluntas beneplaciti* (permission). (2) *Voluntas signi* (precepts and counsels). Hence two general virtues – including all others:– (1) Conformity or Indifference. (2) Obedience (a) to commandments of God and of the Church, (b) to counsels, according to our state, (c) to inspirations, according to supernatural prudence." The first aspect of God's will, "permission", means that we should accept with resignation *all* the circumstances of life, including the unpleasant, the painful, the grievous, and the tragic. We should never be so ungrateful and unjust as to imagine that God actively chooses to bring suffering into our lives. People often speak like that, making God appear to be a monster of cruelty, as if He chose deliberately to unleash wars and famines and plagues on the earth. No, the suffering of humanity is something which God permits, but does not intend. As often as not, human suffering is the result of human sin. Sometimes, as in the case of wars, it is glaringly obvious who is responsible – in other cases it may not be so clear, but if we think about it we can see that the suffering was caused, not by the will of God, but by the selfishness and greed of men. Even an earthquake causes no suffering on its own – it is the falling buildings erected by men that hurt people. Yes, there are cases where we cannot see the human agency behind the suffering, in particular in the case of sickness, where there seems to be no one we can blame except God. Yet we know it is not by God's "precept or counsel" that we should suffer: it is only something that He permits, the suffering must have another source. Since in the great majority of cases we can trace the source of suffering to sin, it is reasonable to suppose that all suffering is caused by the sin of intelligent free beings, even if we cannot see them. It would, after all, be very arrogant to imagine that human beings are the only intelligent creatures around – there are others, and we know, both from the Scriptures and from our own experience, of the suffering the malice of the devil can cause.

God does not directly will suffering, but neither does He simply watch it happening. Whatever happens, He offers a solution. If He permits it, it means that He knows that a greater good can come out of it. More often than we realise, He does quietly intervene to prevent suffering that people would be unable to bear. We can all think of cases of quite remarkable escapes from perils. But not all disasters are averted, great suffering does occur – and in these cases how often we find that people are able to rise to great heights of heroic virtue, acts of unbelievable generosity and kindness, tremendous outpourings of love, which might never have blossomed had there not been the challenge of the circumstances. God permits suffering to happen only when He knows that we are strong enough to bear it, and through bearing it to grow in charity and grace. Not everyone rises to the occasion of course; we all have the freedom and the ability to refuse the opportunity, because to do the will of God must always be our choice at every step of the way. He never forces us, only invites us, cajoles us, yearns for us to respond to His love.

We respond by saying simply, "Thy will be done." That is the simple prayer of Our Lady which began the whole process of our redemption (Luke 1:38). That is the threefold prayer of Our Lord when that redemption was drawing to its consummation. "Not as I will, but as thou wilt." (Matth. 26:39, 42) For Christ came to do the Will of His Father (John 4:34, Heb. 10:5-7). As often as we say, "Thy will be done", we are affirming our desire to be conformed to the will of God, our assent to what He wills for us, our longing to be free from the sin that drags us away from where we truly want to be. As long as we go on repeating those words, we can be certain that we are on the winning side in the long struggle towards holiness. And so Our Lord prays that we should be on His side in our struggle with the world; "As thou didst send me into the world, so I have sent them into the world. And for their sake I consecrate myself, that they also may be consecrated in truth." (John 17:18-19) Putting ourselves on His side means accepting a share in His suffering, His passion which is His compassion for suffering humanity. "Do not be surprised", says St Peter, "at the fiery ordeal which comes upon you, as though something strange were happening to you. But rejoice in so far as you share Christ's sufferings, that you may also rejoice and be glad when his glory is revealed." (1 Peter 4:12-13) That suffering can include the darkness of desolation, the darkness which Christ embraced on the Cross. Mother Teresa was only able to make sense of her own feelings of desolation once she learned to "embrace the darkness".

Until we make that response, God's will is frustrated. "Just as man cannot do any good unless he have the help of God, in the same way God does not work for good in man unless the man consent." (St John Chrysostom) It is up to us, to choose whether to be docile and meek, to model our lives on what we know to be the will of God. Our Lord said, "Blessed are the meek, for they shall inherit the earth." (Matth. 5:5) To be meek, gentle, docile, "mild, obedient, good as He", is to go against the whole drift of the world around us, the world that tells us to be assertive, pushing, confident, and aggressive. And yet the earth is promised to the meek, not the assertive. Even in this world, God keeps His promise – those who antagonise everyone by their brash assertiveness end up losing the friendship and support which might make them happy, while the meek, the self-sacrificing, the generous, the docile, are those who find happiness and spread it around them.

It is so difficult to set ourselves against the mood of the world we live in! Our whole economic system is based on training people to be competitive, to beat down the rival, to establish oneself in first place. Education is directed to the same ends, to prepare children for the mutual aggression of the free market economy. It is hard to step back from all that and say "no" to the ways of the world, to choose to be co-operative and generous. Which is why being "meek" is really very tough indeed. On our own we cannot achieve it; we might like to be docile and obedient, but we find it beyond us. Here is the need for grace, here is the need for that daily prayer "thy will be done", begging God to enable us to resist the powers of the world and to conform ourselves to Him. The promise is that we shall "inherit the earth". That certainly does not mean power, wealth and influence in worldly terms, but it does mean contentment, happiness, a reward in this present life, "manifold more in this time". (Luke 18:30) And it is interesting to see that Pope Benedict includes, in our rightful inheritance of the earth, "the people's right to their own liturgy" (*Jesus of Nazareth*, p. 82). The promise includes contentment in our worship of God, to be able to pray and to develop our Christian life in the Church as Christ intended.

To be "meek" is to model ourselves on Christ. As the Holy Father points out, most of our Bible translations obscure the connection between His meekness and ours, because they do not use the same word, "meek", in the Beatitudes, and in the account of the coming of Christ the King into Jerusalem, "*meek* and riding on an ass" (Zech. 9:9, Matth. 21:5), although the word is the same in the original. He is the true King, whose rule extends over all the earth; if we model ourselves on Him, if we too are "meek", then ours is the earth and all that is in it.

... on earth as it is in heaven.

I understand that phrase, "on earth as it is in heaven", to be intended as the conclusion which embraces the whole of the first half of the Lord's Prayer, asking that the Name be Hallowed, the Kingdom come, the Will be done, "on earth, as it is in heaven." Our mission is to live in this world and to extend the love of God to our neighbour in this world precisely because we are united to Jesus, who Himself is heaven.

When we say "Hallowed be Thy Name on earth, as it is in heaven", we are praying for the extension of the knowledge of God to the entire human race. "For the earth shall be full of the knowledge of the LORD as the waters cover the sea." (Isaiah 11:9) We have a mission, to "make disciples of all nations and baptise them". (Matth. 28:19) Jesus sends us out "like lambs among wolves" (Matth. 10:16), to proclaim the Word, insisting on it, whether people are ready to hear it or not, and to bring them to the point that they desire the Sacraments. If we ever forget that summons to mission, our own faith will weaken, and the Church will dwindle, for mission is of the essence of the faith, the very purpose of the Church.

Our Lord set out at the beginning of His public ministry to visit town after town "to preach there also, for that is why I came." (Mark 1:38) At the very end He summed up His purpose: "I have come into the world to bear witness to the truth." (John 18:37) The Church is Christ's Mystical Body on earth, the union of those who share in His Eucharistic body, and as a body the purpose of the Church must be to continue the work of Christ. "Go into the whole world and preach the gospel to the whole creation." (Mark 16:15) "He who hears you, hears me", "he who believes in me will also do the works that I do." (Luke 10:16, John 14:12) Unless we accept that mission, to do the work of Christ, we cannot claim to be Christ-ians, the Christ-ones.

That mission is daunting, dangerous, difficult. He warns of that very clearly: "I chose you out of the world, therefore the world hates you." (John 15:19) That is why we need to pray every day for the grace to be able to do it, to make His name holy on earth. We cannot do it without His grace; His grace cannot operate in us unless we will it.

In the same way we pray, "Thy kingdom come on earth, as it is in heaven." The meaning of the Kingdom of God is well understood as the Church upon earth, in its many dimensions, but there are other meanings which are also valid. It must refer not only to the invisible spiritual spread of the love of God in the heart, but also to the visible practical spread of the love of neighbour in the hand. Christian charity on the small scale is the little act of kindness, the helpful gesture, the timely gift. On the large scale it is the great charitable works, Christian agencies which feed the multitude of the poor, provide shelter for the homeless, education, employment, nursing and medical care.

On a larger scale still, Christian charity must involve the guidance of the nations in the principles of Catholic social teaching. The Kingdom of God on earth includes efforts towards a just and peaceable human society. The fact that there is at present no evidence that you and I have achieved individual sanctity does not mean that we may stop praying daily for God's kingdom to come about in our hearts; the fact that at present there is no adequate example of a truly Christian state does not in the least excuse us from trying to construct one. The world has suffered for over two hundred years from the blasphemous principle of total separation of Church and state, and the oft-repeated slogan that Christians should keep out of politics. If you stop and think about it for half a minute you will realise that what this really means is that the government of nations should be run exclusively on non-Christian principles, and that Christians should not be allowed even to vote unless they promise to leave their faith behind when they enter the polling booth.

I call this principle "blasphemous" because it is a direct denial that God has any rights over His world, and that the laws of justice and truth which He has revealed may be applied in human affairs. Christians who have an opportunity to take part in public affairs must do so in the spirit of Christian love, otherwise they are tearing themselves in two, and allowing the worse half to exercise power over other people. Of course there are many countries where it is quite impossible for the private citizen to have any influence in public affairs, as was the case in Rome under the emperor Nero. In that case all the Christian can do is to practise charity on the small scale and pray for the enlightenment of the powers. But in countries that pretend to give the citizens the right to express their beliefs, on matters that concern the nation at large, it would be shameful if Christians took no part in public life, and left the running of the nation exclusively to the secular atheists. Taking part in public affairs is called "politics". A Christian who engages in politics must be motivated by the love of God. If that is called "mixing religion and politics", I cannot think of a better way of doing politics. There have in fact been outstanding examples of devout Catholics in public life, who have been motivated by the desire for God's Kingdom in their work for the poor, the oppressed, the downtrodden and the dispossessed, even though many of them have suffered for it. That is not the task of the clergy – that is the role of the laity, but it is a very important part of the Lay Apostolate to strive for the Kingdom of God on earth.

And so we continue, "thy will be done, on earth as it is in heaven." Heaven is where God is, the realm of total unity in the will of God, for it is Our Lord's prayer "that the world may believe that thou hast sent me". (John 17:21) "The essence of heaven is oneness with God's will" (*Jesus of Nazareth*, p. 147). This earth is still the battlefield where we struggle to conform ourselves to the will of God. As long as this life lasts we must continue that struggle, but as long as we never give up we can be absolutely confident we are winning. Never in this life shall we be able to reach the stage of saying, "I have won, I am now totally docile to the Will of God. I am now totally saturated with the love of God, and all who come into contact with me are radiant with love." The more we discover about the love of God the more we realise how very far we still have to go! And in case we should ever be tempted to forget, other people will very quickly remind us of how far we are from being perfected in love for them. But we must never give up praying to be able to do the will of God.

Nor can we ever give up on other people. Our Lord said, "Blessed are the peacemakers, for they shall be called sons of God." (Matth. 5:9) Peace was the first promise made by the angels at Christ's birth, peace was His last bequest to His disciples. We are all invited to be "peacemakers", all invited to become "sons of God". He is Son of God by nature – we are Sons of God by adoption. But of course women and girls are included also, "conformed into the image of His Son", because the most perfect image of Jesus is His blessed Mother.

Peace begins in our own hearts, the peace of knowing that we are at one with God, that we are trying to model our will on His, to bring about His kingdom, to sanctify His name. Then peace grows into the lives of those we meet, our contacts of charity, our words and thoughts of peace towards others. From small beginnings comes peace in our communities, in the places we live and the places we work. From that grows peace in the nation, and from that grows peace between nations. Just as the Kingdom of God has a public, political dimension, so does the work of peace. To be "peacemakers" it may be enough for some to confine themselves to the domestic sphere, to make peace between members of families and between neighbours. But others are called to the larger sphere, and the great work of making peace among warring nations is no less essential a part of our Christian vocation. We cannot claim to be "Sons of God" if we are at war with our brothers, because "anyone who hates his brother is a murderer, and you know that no murderer has eternal life abiding in him". (I John 3:15)

We are obliged, then, by the love of God that dwells in our hearts, to share that love with others. There are times when it is much easier to love our enemies than to love members of our own family, and we may need to practise peacemaking among strangers before we are ready to tackle the most difficult quarrels within the home. But that is something we can never give up: all life long we must struggle for peace, and however futile it appears to be we must never become despondent, for it is His work, the work of grace.

"Peace on earth," sang the angels, "to men of good will". (Luke 2:14) But there are so few men of good will. That is why Our Lord acknowledged in His prayer, "the world has hated them because they are not of the world, even as I am not of the world." (John 17:14) Not even among His own followers would there be peace: "Do you think that I have come to give peace on earth? No, I tell you, but rather division". (Luke 12:51) There are no greater or more intractable divisions than those between people who purport to be followers of Christ. Forty years ago there were great hopes of "reunion" and reconciliation, but they have come to nothing, and where there used to be hundreds of denominations there are now thousands, many of them more bitter and angry against the Church than anything we have seen for centuries. Yet the people who belong to those sects still have the intention of following Christ, however weird a distortion of His truth they have been given! Our love, our efforts for peacemaking, cannot be allowed to cease simply because other people are hostile or suspicious, for "if the world hates you, know that it has hated me before it hated you". (John 15:18) If we wish to be sons of God, we can hardly complain if we are treated in the same way as the incarnate Son of God Himself.

He himself is Peace. His Kingdom is peace; His name is Peace, His will is for our peace. "And His name will be called ... the Prince of Peace." (Isaiah 9:6)

Give us this day our daily Bread ...

Of all the petitions in the Our Father, this seems at first sight to be the most straightforward, yet it is the one that has given rise to the greatest difference of opinion – how should we translate it, to what does it refer? As always, the Catholic answer is that all the possible interpretations are correct, and by looking at them one after another we can come to see something of the astonishing richness of Our Lord's words.

For a start the word "daily" was already causing arguments among the Greeks who read the Gospel in their own language. Both in St Matthew and St Luke the word is *epiousion*, a word found nowhere else in Scripture, or for that matter in all Greek literature before the time of the Gospels. If we take it as a compound word, *ep'-iousion*, it has something to do with what is coming upon us. The simplest translation is "The bread of this day that is now upon us", hence "daily bread". And this meaning is perfectly valid: Our Lord is inviting us to pray for bread, sufficient for the needs of today. Not bread alone, of course (Matth. 4:4), but everything we need for daily life, "your Father knows what you need before you ask Him." (Matth. 6:8) It is "our" bread we ask for, not "mine". We pray together, as a community; we pray for the needs of each other. The last four petitions of the Our Father are all about "us", collectively – we pray for each other, because in this way we fulfil the commandment, "you shall love your neighbour as yourself." (Lev. 19:18) This second Great Commandment sums up the last seven of the Ten Commandments, about how our love of God leads us to love one another.

The basic needs of man are food, clothing and shelter. For these we are entitled to pray, to expect God to preserve His creation. Beyond that is extra, we may enjoy many other good things in this world, and use them for the glory of God and the benefit of our neighbour, but they are not strictly necessary. That is why the Wise Man prays, "give me neither poverty nor riches: feed me with the food that is needful for me." (Prov. 30:8) "If we have food and clothing, with these we shall be content", says St Paul. (I Tim. 6:8)

We need food every day, but we are commanded not to hoard it up for the future. When the Israelites tried to keep back some manna for the next day, they found that it decayed very quickly (Exod. 16:20). The rich man is blamed in the parable for trying to hoard up a vast supply of grain, in the hope of making a profit out of other people's hunger later on (Luke 12:13-21). "Do not be anxious about your life, what you shall eat, or what you shall drink, nor about your body, what you shall put on", said Our Lord; "Do not be anxious about tomorrow, for tomorrow will be anxious for itself. Let the day's own trouble be sufficient for the day." (Matth. 6:25, 34) The rich think they have no worries about the future, the poor know that they must live from day to day. The words of the Our Father remind us that we must identify ourselves as poor, the "poor in spirit", the "poor of the LORD".

We are, then, encouraged to ask our Father with full confidence for the needs of our daily life. We are not encouraged to go on about them, to detail in long eloquent discourses exactly what we think we need. God offers us what we need, which is not necessarily what we think we need. "What man among you, if his son asks him for bread, will give him a stone? Or if he asks for a fish, will give him a serpent?" (Matth. 7:9-10) The problem is, left to ourselves, we will persist in asking for stones and serpents. If we make up our own petitions, and give God a Christmas list of things we want, and which we have convinced ourselves we need, we will inevitably be asking for all the wrong things, things which it would be disastrous for us to have. Children frequently demand things of us which would be dangerous, distasteful or doubtful: we try to please them by giving them something they really ought to like much better, but they are never grateful. No matter how tasty the fish we offer them, they would much rather have a snake to play with. None of us are any better than children in this respect, which is why in all our prayers of petition, as we have observed already, we must be honest enough to recognise that God knows what is good for us far better than we ever possibly could, and that what He does give us is the best for us in the circumstances of today.

But having said all that, some of the Greeks pointed out that the word *ep'-iousion*, something to do with what is coming upon us, might just as easily mean "for the day that is coming", in other words "for tomorrow". Does that contradict everything we have just been saying about having no concern for the morrow, and not trying to keep our manna fresh till the next morning? No, once we remember that the word "day" has a more profound meaning in Scripture than a mere passage of twenty-four hours. The most common interpretation of the "days of creation" among the early Fathers of the Church, and for that matter among many of the Rabbis of Our Lord's own time, was that each "day" represents a "thousand years". Nor did they mean a literal "1,000 years" either it represented a "long time" or even a "geological age" (II Peter 3:8, cf. Newman, *Via Media*, II, p. 321). Specifically, many of the Fathers understood that the whole of the period from the beginning until the Incarnation of Christ was the first five Days, and that the Sixth Day, the day of the creation of the Son of Man, begins with the birth of Our Lord. We are still in that Sixth Day – the Sabbath is yet to come. The Coming Day, the day of rest, will not dawn until the harvest is ripe, but it will be the "Day of the Lord" as promised (or threatened) by the Prophets. On that interpretation, we are praying for the Bread from Heaven which is also our Bread for Heaven, the Bread which will sustain us for the coming of the Last Day.

And the children of Israel found that if they preserved manna for the Sabbath Day it did keep perfectly well (Exod. 16:23-5).

In this context we can let the Greeks confuse us even more by pointing out that the word *epiousion* can be divided differently: if it is really *epi-ousion*, it means something like "above or beyond being or substance." St Jerome, who knew Greek and Hebrew well, hedged his bets by translating it "daily" (*quotidianum*) in St Luke, and "super-substantial" (*supersubstantialem*) in St Matthew. In the latter case he comments that it means "outstanding" or "very excellent", and proceeds naturally to observe that "that which is above all substance is the Body of the Lord." In other words *epiousion* can effectively mean "trans-substantial". The substance or "being" of the bread is transformed, we are begging for what looks like bread but is in reality of a different substance, the Body of Christ. The majority of the Church Fathers saw this petition as essentially eucharistic (*Jesus of Nazareth*, p. 154).

We are praying, therefore, for the Bread of Life, the Blessed Sacrament. That is the ultimate gift Christ has for us, His own Body, given to us by the Father, through the invocation of the Holy Spirit. As we pray in the Mass (Eucharistic Prayer III), "Therefore, O Lord, we humbly implore you, graciously make holy by the same Spirit, these gifts we have brought to you for consecration, that they may become the Body and Blood of your Son our Lord, Jesus Christ." We pray to the Father that the Holy Spirit will come on our gifts to transform them (trans-substantiate, *epi-ousion*), to become the Bread which feeds us in our spiritual life every day (daily, *ep'-iousion*), and prepares us for the dawning of the Day to come. It is Holy Communion that makes us one with Christ, and therefore identified with Him in His Son-ship; it is Holy Communion that anticipates in us the life of the world to come, it is the Bread of Heaven, that Heaven which now is, already among us though unseen.

That we should receive Holy Communion every day is also legitimately drawn from the interpretation "daily bread". Our human nature being frail as it is, we need to be revived every day, to make a fresh start every morning. We cannot rely on the love and devotion we felt yesterday to carry us over to tomorrow. If we are unable to receive Holy Communion every day, God's grace is more than sufficient to bridge the gaps, but if we have the opportunity to receive Him, and fail to do so, then we can hardly be surprised if love begins to grow cold within us. The one petition embraces all the possible meanings and profundities of Our Lord's Eucharistic teaching, as we find it in chapter six of St John's Gospel. There is earthly food, there is the manna from heaven, there is the flesh of Jesus Christ. "Thou hast given him power over all flesh, to give eternal life to all whom thou hast given him." (John 17:2)

Our Lord said, "Blessed are those who hunger and thirst for righteousness, for they shall be satisfied." (Matth. 5:6) "Righteousness", which can also be "justice" in some translations, represents one of the great terms of the Old Testament which has many meanings – and as usual we can welcome every one of them as valid, and true in this context. To begin with, "righteousness" is not an abstract thing or idea, it is a Person. He himself is the Righteousness that is rained down from the heavens, as Isaiah sang, "Shower, O heavens, from above, and let the skies rain down righteousness." (Isaiah 45:8) The Fathers always understood this as a direct prophecy of the coming of Christ, who is the Righteous One, the Just One. In our hunger and thirst we are longing, yearning for Him, just as the prophets and sages of the Old Testament all yearned to see Him. "Your father Abraham rejoiced that he was to see my day; he saw it and was glad." (John 8:56) All those who seek Him will surely find Him, so that our desire for Him will certainly be satisfied. All those who yearn for the truth are already on their way to Christ, whether they know His name or not. "All that the Father gives to me will come to me, and him who comes to me I will not cast out." "If a man loves me he will keep my word, and my Father will love him, and we will come to him and make our home with him." "Sanctify them in the truth; thy word is truth." (John 6:37, 14:23, 17:17)

Righteousness as a word was originally "right-wise-ness", the quality of being at rights with God. That is also what we call "justification". We desire, we hunger and thirst to be at rights with God, for that is the great work of our redemption. We are no longer estranged, separated from God by the huge gulf which sunders Creator from creation: we are one with Him through our Eucharistic union with Jesus his Son. St Paul imagines the whole of creation groaning as it strives upwards towards God (Rom. 8:22), but God has come down into His creation, and His creature, Mary, has given birth to the One who unites heaven and earth. In Him is our justification, our righteousness. We are at one with God, and our hunger is satisfied.

But "righteousness" also means the effect that this oneness with God must have in our lives: there can be no justification without also sanctification, for unless we deliberately refuse the work of grace, our contact with the love of God will inevitably transform us. That transformation is what makes us "righteous", turns us into the sort of people we were originally intended to be. All virtues are comprised in that one word "righteousness", but the whole of virtue is given in the one gift of charity. If we have charity, the love of God, rooted in our hearts, then we shall find the other virtues follow in her train. If only we "hunger and thirst" for that righteousness, if we truly want to be transformed by the love of God, then we shall be satisfied.

And the effect of that righteousness which is granted to us must be shown in our love for others. We cannot keep the love of God to ourselves, it must overflow and spread out to everyone we meet. For that reason the "hunger and thirst for righteousness" must include a burning desire to meet the sorrows of people in the world, to relieve suffering and bring gladness to the distressed. The hunger for justice must include social justice, the Kingdom of God on earth. The social teaching of the Catholic Church has never been more relevant than today, and we must never allow the occasional minutiae in emphasis to deter us from attempting to put it into practice. (Recent Papal teaching on social justice is summarised in Rodger Charles SJ, *An Introduction to Catholic Social Teaching,* Family Publications 1999.) Yet here, alas, experience shows that in this life we will never be truly satisfied. Even if we devote our whole lives to efficient work for the relief of suffering, there will still be injustice and distress in the world. As long as this world lasts, we will still see the wicked living prosperously and dying with honour, while the poor are trampled and justice is never granted them. Zophar the Naamathite claimed that "the exalting of the wicked is short, and the joy of the godless but for a moment... his prosperity will not endure", but Job sensibly pointed out that "the wicked reach old age and grow mighty in power, their children are established in their presence... their houses are safe from fear." (Job 20:5, 21; 21:7, 9) We do not see justice done on earth, and it is no use pretending that we do. The fulfillment of that beatitude, therefore, must point beyond this life to the Day that is to come, the new life for which we are prepared by the Bread of Heaven.

We may note in passing that whereas in the Prayer Our Lord speaks only of "bread", in the beatitudes He speaks of hunger and also of thirst. It is very curious how the mention of thirst and drink is so much less prominent in Our Lord's words than that of hunger and food, and the Bread come down from heaven. In that great Eucharistic discourse at Capernaum (John, chapter 6), Our Lord speaks at great length about eating His Body, after the miracle which involves bread and fishes but no wine – and then almost as an afterthought appears the mention of drinking His blood (verses 53-6 only). In St Matthew and St Mark we hear how He institutes the Eucharist under the forms of bread and wine – but the wine is omitted from many manuscripts of St Luke, and is certainly not mentioned in the clearly Eucharistic supper at Emmaus (Luke 24:30-35). Nor do we ever hear of wine in the Acts of the Apostles, which speaks often of the "breaking of bread". What we may legitimately conclude is that the practice of the Catholic Church down the ages has not been incorrect: Holy Communion is normally given under the form of bread, but on certain rare occasions is also given under the form of wine. As the Catechism so clearly states, Our Lord is received whole and entire under either species (CCC 1390). We may "hunger and thirst", but both are satisfied when we receive our Daily Bread.

... and forgive us our trespasses, as we forgive those who trespass against us ...

It is perhaps unfortunate that despite the fact that during the last generation virtually every other form of prayer was changed beyond recognition, we still preserve unchanged the extraordinary word "trespasses". Especially as, according to Fr Thurston (*Familiar Prayers*, 1953, p. 33), the word was first chosen for the English version promulgated by King Henry VIII! The old Scots version is much better: "Forgi'e us our debts, as we forgi'e our debtors". Which is what the Greek actually says. Our Lord expanded this idea in the great parable of the debts, the man who owed his master ten thousand talents – a Barings Bank sort of debt – and would not forgive his fellow a hundred denarii (Matth. 18:23-35). The word "trespasses" has very little meaning in English (or Scots) and rather tends to conceal the full dramatic force of Our Lord's words. Not only does He challenge us to forgive each other's debts, He also puts

115

it in the past tense, for in St Matthew's Gospel the Greek text really reads "forgive us our debts *to the extent that we have forgiven* those who were in debt to us." To be technical, it is a "perfect" tense, *aphékamen,* meaning that the action is done and completed: dare we say that we have completed our intention of forgiving others? It is a little softer in St Luke, as we might expect, an "imperfect" tense, *aphiemen,* something we have been working on but may not yet have quite completed. And St Luke uses the word "sins" rather than "debts". But in either case we are committing ourselves to having at least begun to forgive those in debt to us. When we pray we are actually committing ourselves to the forgiveness of others as a condition of the forgiveness we want for ourselves.

The "Debts" in the parable of the unforgiving debter means everything we owe to God, all our obligations to Him. In the first place it means the debt we owe Him for creation itself: "for what have you that you did not receive?" (I Cor. 4:7) Everything we are, and everything we have, is a gift from God. We cannot possibly pay Him back for that, even assuming He might require it at our hands. We do not presume to ask our children to repay us for giving them birth, for educating them and equipping them for life. That applies to spiritual children as much as biological children! If we have been privileged to give life, to teach knowledge and skills, to preach the Word of God and instruct many in the ways of God, all that is no more than passing on a little of what God has given us. "You received without paying, give without pay", says Our Lord. (Matth. 10:8) We pray that God will continue to give freely, and in so doing we are praying that He will enable us to be generous in giving to others.

The Debt also includes the continuous daily flow of Grace that makes it possible for us to live and grow in virtue. We can do nothing good except at the initiative, the invitation, of God: we can exercise no virtue, no talent, no ability, without the constant support of grace. Left to ourselves we would disintegrate immediately, for without His love we cannot exist, let alone "live and move and have our being". (Acts 17:28) He claims nothing from us in exchange for all that − except to treat others with equal generosity. "Love one another, as I have loved you." (John 15:12)

All this huge debt to God would still exist even in an unfallen state, and we must not forget that debt, for creation and for grace. God "forgives" it, He does not expect any return for it, other than the return of love for others; even from the Cherubim who stand glorious before Him, even from Our Lady who was the first to acknowledge her debt to God for the grace with which she was filled, "for he who is mighty has done great things for me". (Luke 1:49) Similarly, others would incur a debt to us even if they and we were perfect and sinless. Our Lady could pray in the words of the Our Father and this phrase would not be meaningless for her.

But we live in a fallen world, and our debts to God are that much greater in consequence. The most immediate meaning of this invocation in the Our Father is the remission of sins. (That may be what Henry VIII was thinking of − God knows he had need enough of it −

117

when he narrowed the petition to speak of "trespasses", which does mean literally "offences" or "going out of bounds".) When we pray the Our Father we pray every day for the forgiveness of sins, and we commit ourselves to forgiving the sins of others.

We cannot omit this aspect of the Prayer, we may never be so foolish as to imagine we do not need to have our sins forgiven, as Our Lord makes abundantly clear when He adds, immediately after giving us the Prayer: "For if you forgive men their trespasses, your heavenly Father also will forgive you; but if you do not forgive men their trespasses, neither will your Father forgive your trespasses." (Matth. 6:14-15) In the version preserved by St Luke we hear "forgive us our sins, for we ourselves forgive everyone who is indebted to us." (Luke 11:4)

St Augustine seized on this passage in his controversy against the Pelagians, who imagined that it was possible for someone to avoid sin by his own sheer strength of character, without the help of God. The fact that we are all commanded to pray for forgiveness from sin, means that we must all admit we are sinners, and that it is impossible for us to avoid sin except through grace. "If we say we have no sin, we deceive ourselves, and the truth is not in us." (I John 1:8) But the extreme Augustinians also need to be corrected, those who flatter themselves that once they have received the formal stamp of grace and are assured of salvation, they can never sin again, or if they do it does not matter. Despite the grace that God does undoubtedly give us, we, being fallible weak human creatures, constantly fail to make full use of that grace, and our sins and failings do matter. Our Lord not only called His apostles, but continued to maintain them in that call, even though one insisted on using his free will to betray Him. "While I was with them, I kept them in thy name, which thou hast given me; I have guarded them, and none of them is lost but the son of perdition." (John 17:12) Yes, we have been baptised and saved, but we are still going to go on failing again and again, as St John Chrysostom pointed out, "it is necessary for sins to be forgiven, even after baptism." We need the simple honesty to look at our lives, every day, and to admit that we need God's forgiveness, every day. "A righteous man falls seven times", says King Solomon, "and rises again". (Prov. 24:16)

The Sacrament of Penance is of course one of God's greatest gifts to fallen humanity, the opportunity to return again and again to Our Father and to hear the voice of the Church speaking with the authority of Christ, "Take heart, my son, your sins are forgiven." (Matth. 9:2) The debt of our sins has been paid for us by Our Lord on the Cross; all we need do is claim that redemption through the sacrament He instituted for us. But between confessions we can recite the Our Father frequently with that simple confidence of forgiveness for our frequent imperfections, our failures in charity, our falling short in the ultimate challenge to love with whole heart and soul and mind.

And then we look at the way others behave towards us. Is there any limit on the forgiveness of God? There is no limit either on the forgiveness we owe to our

119

neighbour. "Then Peter came up and said to him, 'Lord, how often shall my brother sin against me, and I forgive him? As many as seven times?' Jesus said to him, 'I do not say to you seven times, but seventy times seven.' " (Matth. 18:21-2) Was St Peter irritated by some mistake his brother Andrew had made seven times, something to do with the fishing boat or the nets? So often it is the little irritating things that the people closest to us do which are so difficult to forgive. Forgiving our real enemies can be very much easier than forgiving our closest friends, our "brother".

That dialogue with St Peter is the introduction to the parable about the debts, but it follows a passage where Our Lord implies that there may be a limit to forgiveness. That is the passage beginning, "if your brother sins against you, go and tell him his fault…" (Matth. 18:15-20) In that case, after the brother has been challenged once alone, once before witnesses, and once before the community, but still will not listen, then "treat him as a Gentile and a tax-collector". What is the point here? Simply that the brother will not ask for forgiveness, nor admit his fault. We are not obliged to forgive those who do not repent, do not ask for forgiveness, and remain obstinate in their attitude of defiance. Someone who has hurt us deeply, and shows absolutely no remorse, no flicker of regret, no attempt to ask our forgiveness does not get forgiven. When we say – and it is good if we can say it – "I forgive you", to those who attack us without remorse, that forgiveness cannot really take effect until they accept it. We must hold ourselves in readiness to forgive, so that what we mean by "I forgive you" is really,

"If you were to repent, I would forgive you, and I pray that God will forgive you." More than that is not possible – and even to get to that stage may need many recitals of the Our Father before God's grace has softened us. But to that state we must aspire, we must always be ready to forgive as soon as they ask for forgiveness, to pray for their forgiveness before God even if we have lost touch with them completely, or if they have died. We may never bolt the door of our heart, so that if they come a-knocking we can open to them at once.

We should remember that God also is not obliged to forgive those who do not repent, do not ask for forgiveness, and remain obstinate in their attitude of defiance. Those who do not want to enter Heaven are not compelled.

Our Lord said, "Blessed are the merciful, for they shall obtain mercy." (Matth. 5:7) God revealed Himself in the very beginning as a God who is "merciful and gracious, slow to anger and abounding in steadfast love." (Exod. 34:6) He revealed Himself in the fulness of time as God with us, Emmanuel, the God who is on our side against the world (Matth. 1:23). He reveals Himself every day as the God whose mercy in our hearts causes us to be merciful to those around us. At the very end He will reveal Himself as the God who requires an account of the mercy we have shown to others as the measure of his mercy to us. "As you did it to one of the least of these my brethren, you did it to me." (Matth. 25:40) The quality of mercy is infinite: there is no limit to the extent to which God will remit our debts, will forgive our sins, will cancel the bill He could hold against us – but over and over again Our Lord returns in His teaching, in His parables, to the requirement for us to be as long-suffering and compassionate towards those that have hurt us, those in debt to us, those who do not deserve our love. "For with the judgment you pronounce you will be judged, and the measure you give will be the measure you get." (Matth. 7:2)

But what a consoling doctrine that is! If we look back at the long sordid tangled record of our past blunders and meannesses and petty malice, and our hearts faint with embarrassment and fear, with the guilt that makes us want to hide our faces in decent company; if we look at the unutterable perfection of holiness as we see it in the lives of the greater saints, and shudder at the immense gap that lies between us and them; if we feel that even if Our Lord were to open the gate of heaven wide and beckon us in, we would shrink with shame at the thought of defiling that heaven with our muddy footprints, "take me away, and in the lowest deep there let me be ..." (Newman, *Dream of Gerontius*) – why then, all we have to do is to think of those who are in debt to us, and make a firm resolution to want to love them, to be ready to forgive them, to desire to show mercy to them! If we know that we have tried to forgive others, we can be quite certain that God will succeed in forgiving us.

... and lead us not into temptation ...

This is a puzzling phrase, "shocking", even. How can we imagine that God will *lead* us into temptation? It is tempting to change the text, to turn it into a duplicate of the next petition and pray simply that God will protect us from temptation, as in fact the common Spanish translation of the Our Father actually does. But we are not entitled to do that: the text is quite clear, and it is the same in both St Matthew and St Luke. *Do not ... lead us ... into temptation.* We must pray the Prayer and let God speak to us through the words He has actually given us, not the words we would like to put into His mouth. And the words were carefully chosen – a point we had all missed, until the Pope pointed it out, is that only a couple of pages before St Matthew had used exactly the same phrase about Our Lord, "Jesus was *led* up by the Spirit *into* the wilderness to be *tempted*...". (Matth. 4:1, cf. Luke 4:1-2, and *Jesus of Nazareth*, p. 161) In our interpretation of this phrase of the Our Father we must not ignore that reference.

What then do we mean by "temptation". As ever, there are several meanings, all of which are valid. The most common use of the word is to refer to interior temptations to sin. None of us can pretend that we do not feel incessantly tempted by sins, of one sort or another, and the worst temptations to the most embarrassing sins are the ones that sweep through the mind just when we are trying to pray. Different people, of course, are tempted by different sins: something which one person may feel is the bugbear of his life may not occur to another person at all. There are ten commandments, not just one, and most people pass on eight or nine of them. But naturally we are most concerned, most anxious, over the one that happens to affect us. Moreover, we feel that everyone else must know about it, and we imagine that they are all watching us, and sighing knowingly to themselves when they see us distracted at Mass; they must be aware of what we were thinking of, and how they must despise us! And all the while those other people are feeling equally embarrassed about their private temptations which are quite different from ours.

Temptations change as we get older, too. Perhaps children are most bothered by greed, young people by lust, the middle aged by the love of money, the old by pride and the desire for power. These are progressively more serious sins. But we can never imagine that we have ever grown out of previous temptations: they can always return unexpectedly! Temptation is part of the human condition. That is why Our Lord had to experience temptation Himself, "who in every respect has been tempted as we are, yet without sin". (Heb. 4:15) Temptation is not, in itself, a sin. Indeed, a temptation is an excellent occasion for growth in grace and the love of God. If, as often as we are tempted, we turn to God in a quick aspiration of prayer, and if we use the recollection of that temptation as a reminder to ourselves not to become complacent or proud, why then we are better off as a result of the struggle with temptation than if we had never been stirred at all.

So why do we pray that God will not lead us into such temptations? Simply because we should never be so arrogant as to imagine that we will deal with them successfully. We may not challenge the Spirit to treat us as He treated Our Lord. As St Cyprian says on this passage, "let no one put himself forward insolently". We must not ask God to set us a challenge; we must not offer ourselves for a struggle in the conceited over-confidence that we will conquer. What we are asking in this prayer is that God will restrain us from such pride, from the sin of presumption. That His love will make us sufficiently humble, so that we will not "tempt the LORD our God". (Matth. 4:7) Because if we rush headlong into temptations, it is God that we are putting to the test – we are challenging Him to exert His special protecting grace, to send an angel especially to strengthen us, to work miracles for our own glory, to enable us to shrug off the temptation with a prayer. The angels, we are told, did not "minister" to Our Lord until after He had seen off the devil (Matth. 4:11), for Jesus by His very nature has a strength that we may not presume to claim.

Having said that, the same principle applies to the other meanings of "temptation", which are the greater challenges to our faith, our perseverance and our charity. The trials or temptations which come on the faithful Christian are not only internal, but often external, the difficulties of life, and in particular the difficulties brought upon us by other people. In the face of adversity, our faith is tested. We do not know how well we should do under adversity, though God does know, and He often does allow us to suffer these trials, just as Job suffered the assaults of Satan, so that we ourselves may discover how strong we are capable of being. It is the greatest saints who are tested most, but we should not presume we are in their class.

Of all trials and temptations, in this sense of the word, the ultimate is persecution for the Faith. At no time in the history of the Church has there been total freedom from persecution, though the century just past was the period of the greatest and most sustained of all. More martyrs died in the twentieth century than in all the previous ages of the Faith – the century that prided itself on being enlightened, tolerant and liberal. When we hear the stories of the martyrs, and listen to what the survivors tell us of the difficult times, we are amazed at the heroic perseverance displayed by ordinary, unassuming people. We are dismayed, also, by the lack of courage shown by the confident and strong. My mother always said that of her acquaintance the ones who withstood torture best were the quiet intellectuals, not the burly strong men, just as the burly fisherman St Peter denied Our Lord while the willowy St John stood by Him.

Which of us can dare to say that we would be among the valiant? We may not presume on our own courage or steadfastness: that is why we pray, "lead us not into temptation". We may ask not to be put to the test, indeed Our Lord commands us to "watch and pray that you may not enter into temptation." (Matth. 26:41) We hear stories of self-confident Christians, in antiquity and in more recent persecutions, who deliberately ran themselves into danger, and boldly challenged the authorities. Not all of them eventually stood firm in the test they had so rashly set themselves, and the Church has always been reluctant to call them martyrs. St Teresa tells us of how she and her brother once ran away from home in the hope of being martyred – but she tells it as an example of childish folly. (*Life*, I,4) St Cyprian, whom I quoted earlier, had no hesitation in running away when persecution began, and even wrote a little pamphlet to explain why he was right to do so. Eventually they caught up with him, and he went heroically to his martyrdom, but ever since then Christians under persecution have known that they should do everything they can to avoid danger, without compromising on the truth. Hence the hair-raising but often amusing escapes – a classic story recently reprinted is that of John Gerard who safely got away from the Tower of London. He missed being a martyr, and therefore canonised, but lived to train many in the ways of virtue. (*John Gerard: the Autobiography of an Elizabethan*, Family Publications 2006)

In one way or another, the faith of every one of us must be tested, for we never grow except in the face of a challenge. St Augustine's comment on this passage is to the effect that no one can prove himself except under trial, but to be "led into temptation means that trials come which we cannot bear." Against such challenges we can confidently pray God will defend us.

St James reassures us about the nature of temptations, in more than one sense of the word: firstly he says, "count it all joy, my brethren, when you meet various trials" (Jam. 1:2), because without these challenges our faith will never grow. We are set upon this earth to learn to love, and without these difficult exercises in loving other people, we shall never learn. Difficulties, whether they are brought on us by our enemies or our friends and family, are the background to our continuing growth in love. "Blessed," therefore, "is the man who endures trial"

(Jam. 1:12). He goes on to talk about interior temptations, firstly warning us against making the common mistake that it is God who tempts us to evil, "for God cannot be tempted with evil and he himself tempts no one." (Jam. 1:13) Temptations of that inner sort come from our own desires: what comes from God is "every good endowment and every perfect gift". (Jam. 1:17)

Despite those clear words in Scripture, Christians often fall into the error of imagining that it is God who brings down evil and sorrow upon us, or who inserts desires for evil within us. That is not true: the sorrows and woes and griefs of this world are not directly willed by God, though He does permit them if He knows that we will be able to withstand them, and can even profit from them. In the same way internal temptations to sin derive from our own desires, what the Church calls Original Sin: God permits them to challenge us only because He also gives us the grace to resist them, and thus to grow in perfection as a result. We may feel we would rather choose our own challenges, and like St Paul we may beseech the Lord about our temptations that they should leave us (cf. II Cor 12:8), but a temptation of our own choosing will never be anything like so valuable an opportunity for growth in love as those which circumstances bring upon us.

St Paul cheers us up: "No temptation has overtaken you that is not common to man. God is faithful, and He will not let you be tempted beyond your strength, but with the temptation will also provide the way of escape, that you may be able to endure it." (I Cor. 10:13) Our temptations are "common to man", merely human, not like the temptations of Christ. When we pray "lead us not into temptation" we are asking God to fill us with the confidence to believe that we can always survive whatever temptations come upon us. There are, of course, many occasions when God does intervene to protect us, when He knows that we are too frail to endure. But such occasions are almost impossible to detect, and we hardly ever reflect on the times when, surprisingly, we have *not* been tempted.

There remains the final temptation, the Great Trial which heralds the End. Our Lord speaks of this in figurative language, and uses many different parables to indicate the manner in which we are to make our final choice for Him or against Him. But He also warns us severely against trying to predict the time of the End, still more against trying to hasten it on. The world is His field, full of good and bad alike, and so it will remain until the Harvest. Our task is to live in it now. Many of the great events of history have been foreshadowings or pre-echoes of the End, and for those caught up in them the choices have been stark, to love God or to reject Him. In times of comparative peace the petty little challenges of every-day charity can be even more difficult to meet. In all these events we continue to pray that God will not allow us to fall under temptations too heavy for us to bear, and since that prayer is dictated to us by Christ Himself, we can be confident in the expectation of sufficient grace. "My grace is sufficient for you, for my power is made perfect in weakness." (II Cor. 12:9)

Our Lord also said, "Blessed are those who mourn, for they shall be comforted." (Matth. 5:4) We are tempted to complain, to grieve, to "mourn" even, because of the temptations or trials that come upon us. We look at the appalling way in which our country is misgoverned (any country, it doesn't matter where you're reading this), and we cry out in anger at a God who can allow it. We look at the squalour and poverty of so many good people living just across the railway tracks from us, and blame God angrily for our own failure to do something about it, or for their failure to be touchingly grateful for the help we give them, and to reform their lives immediately. We look at the ravages of disease destroying those we love before our eyes, and we are so angry with God that we try to threaten Him by declaring He doesn't exist. So often our "mourning" is compassion, grieving because of the suffering of others, just as Our Lady mourned beside the Cross.

We may "mourn" also because of the afflictions that come upon ourselves. Even if we are sanguine and philosophical about great external trials, we can be consumed with rage at the way our mother-in-law behaves towards us. Or we can be grieved excessively by small things in the privacy of our own rooms. Cassian writes about his time as a holy hermit in the desert, with no one around him, and no news of the wicked world to disturb his tranquillity, how "we can remember becoming vexed with a pen, whether it was too fine or too broad; with the penknife, whose edge was too blunt to cut cleanly." (*The Monastic Institutes* VIII, 19) (Can you imagine how vexed he would have been with a computer?) Wherever we live, whatever we do, no matter with what safeguards we surround ourselves, there will always be irritations, inconveniences, awkward people, badly-behaved objects, to grieve us, to "tempt" us or try us, to test our patience, our kindness, our love.

Then there is the "mourning" we feel when we reflect on our own weakness, our inadequacy, our sins, the "mourning occasioned by the shattering encounter with truth". (*Jesus of Nazareth*, p. 86) We weep for our own sins, like Mary Magdalen weeping at Our Lord's feet (Luke 7:38), knowing how much God has loved us, and how little we have done to return that love, or reflect it into the lives of others.

And in every case, God will infallibly give us the grace we need to comfort us. "Your faith has saved you, go in peace." (Luke 7:50) The very first man to cry out under the weight of temptation was Cain, "My punishment is greater than I can bear", and the LORD comforted him with the mark, "lest any who came upon him should kill him." (Gen. 4:13, 15) When Job and his friends had filled thirty seven chapters with poetic complaint, the LORD gives him His answer, and Job finds his comfort in the realisation "I know that thou canst do all things, and that no purpose of thine can be thwarted." (Job 42:1) In different ways, after different trials, it is always possible to come to that realisation – that God does in fact love us, and that ultimately everything that happens can be turned to good. "That they may have my joy fulfilled in themselves ... that the love with which thou hast loved me may be in them, and I in them." (John 17:13, 26) "In everything God works for good with those who love Him" (Rom. 8:28). "All shall be well, and all shall be well, and all manner of thing shall be well." (Julian of Norwich, *Revelations of Divine Love*, chapter 27)

... but deliver us from evil.

And so at last we come to that final prayer for protection, a prayer we can be confident God will grant us since we know it is His will that we ask it. In one sense it is included in the previous petition, which is why it is omitted in the version given by St Luke, but it reminds us again of Our Lord's temptation in the desert by the Evil One. Protection He will give, if only we ask for it, but unless we ourselves want to be protected from evil, not all the legions of angels can deliver us. Our Lord renounced His right to that protection, because it was His will to suffer the worst that evil could bring upon Him – "Do you think that I cannot appeal to my Father, and He will at once send me more than twelve legions of angels?" (Matth. 26:53) He would not allow His human followers to defend Him either, but went to His death defenceless as a Lamb. We on the other hand may not renounce our rights in the same way, we may not dare to challenge evil unprotected. Just as the last petition prayed that we would not be tested like Jesus in the desert, so now we pray not to be handed over into the power of the evil one as Our Lord was handed over.

We are commanded to pray "deliver us from evil", because we are too weak, too unreliable to be trusted. By this prayer we are forced to admit that we cannot trust ourselves. If we were unprotected when we were confronted with evil, we would fall at once. We do indeed fall often, precisely because we neglect to pray, or because our prayer is at best half-hearted. We recite the words, but at the back of the mind is still an unspoken longing to surrender to evil. Half-hearted, luckily, for we do not surrender totally to evil, nor are we fully aware of what we are doing, we do not give our full consent to evil. But that half consent, that weakness of will which deprives the prayer of its full effect, that is what lets sin and evil into our lives. And so we have to go back and pray again for forgiveness, every day.

What, then is evil? The Church fathers agree, when commenting on this passage, that evil is not a mere abstraction, it is a person. Both in Greek and in Latin it is impossible to tell from the words whether we are praying for liberation from "evil" in the neuter, or from "the evil one" in the masculine (*a malo, apo tou ponérou*). St John Chrysostom says bluntly, "here by the evil one he means the devil." Some modern translations have made this explicit, but in any case it is necessary to know that "we are not contending against flesh and blood, but against the Principalities, against the Powers". (Eph. 6:12) There are malicious beings around us, and their influence in one way or other is always for our harm. There are benevolent beings around us, and their influence, directed by the will of God, is always for our protection and our happiness. We must not forget the explicit teaching of Our Lord that even the least of us have angels continually in the presence of our Father in heaven.

We recognise the existence of the Evil One, but we are not to pay any attention to him. The impulses to evil within us, which we call interior "temptations", derive ultimately from the Evil One, but more immediately from our own desires and hidden vices. We should not waste time probing into them, or incite them by too much introspection. Our protection against them comes in many forms, and our co-operation with that protection involves an acceptance of the assistance provided. If we want to be delivered from the evil within us, God will prompt us to innocent thoughts. "Whatever is true, whatever is honourable, whatever is just, whatever is pure, whatever is lovely, whatever is gracious", says St Paul, "think about these things". (Phil. 4:8) If we have something good to think about, evil will find less of a foothold. That is why St Philip used to recommend light reading, books of innocent jokes, to occupy the mind so that there is less room for distracting thoughts that so easily tend towards evil. Sometimes it is easier to fill the mind with honest entertainment than with profound thoughts of sublime divinity!

The attacks of the Evil One come upon us also from outside, in the innumerable accidents of life, and the limitless malice of our enemies. Even here God's protection is all around us, but so often we do not notice it. In the classic Roman liturgy the last petition of the Our Father is expanded into the prayer *libera nos*, asking God to protect us from all evils, past, present and to come. Confident in the shelter of His wings we can walk unafraid in the dark places of the earth. It is with this divine confidence that the martyrs faced persecution and death. The angels keep their ancient places, they extend their protection to us even in the material things of this world. It is rare that we observe their passing, for when everything goes well for us, we take it for granted. That we should not do – one aspect of this prayer must surely be to give thanks for the deliverance from evil we experience day after day. How often we travel, without incident or accident, sometimes even without delay! How often we find that we have walked unharmed through places where strong men fear to tread and the police dare not go at all! How often we spend a whole day without serious illness or injury! We are very quick indeed to point out to our guardian angels when something has gone wrong, and we may even blame their negligence, but we never give thanks when things go well.

Yes, accidents and attacks do happen, and illness and decay are all round us. Few are so weak that they need to be protected from evil totally all their life long: most of us have sufficient strength of character that God can see that we are capable of profiting from a little adversity. Under strict controls the Evil One is occasionally allowed to give us the opportunity of showing what we are made of (cf. Job 1:12). That is why deliverance from "evil" does not always include deliverance from "evils", the bad things that happen to us which give us the opportunity to grow in grace. We have already seen that God will never allow us to be tempted beyond our capabilities, and we can be sure that He will continue to guard and protect us even during the most extreme conditions of trial. Our Lord prays for us:

"I do not pray that thou shouldst take them out of the world, but that thou shouldst keep them from the evil one." (John 17:15) We too must do our part: we must continue to pray "deliver us from evil", and we must never imagine that we are capable of resisting evil by our own strength. All our strength, all our protection, comes from God. Our part is simply to ask for it.

Our Lord said, "Blessed are those who are persecuted for righteousness' sake, for theirs is the kingdom of heaven." (Matth. 5:10) We are taught to pray that we be not persecuted, to ask God to deliver us from evil and the evil one, and to protect us against all harm – but the fact remains that many people, good people, people who pray the Our Father with sincerity and devotion, do find themselves being persecuted. Suffering comes upon all of us in little ways, but on some it comes in great ways, even to the point of death, death on a cross. And so often we suffer precisely because we are trying to do what is right. Just as Our Lord suffered for bringing righteousness into the world.

We have a promise that God will not permit anyone to be tested beyond their endurance, but very many have been put to death for their endurance. There need be no anxiety about this – God has not forgotten His promises, and the unmerited suffering of the good is no threat to our understanding of the goodness of God, for He clearly, precisely, and repeatedly told us that it would happen.

The word "persecution" has acquired a somewhat technical sense, to mean the organised oppression of the faith by state authority, but in origin the word has a much wider scope. It includes King Herod's mad attack on the infant Christ (Matth. 2:16-18). It can include the dishevelled enraged mob which hustled Our Lord out of the synagogue and somehow let him slip away in the chaos (Luke 4:28-30). It can include the relentless hostility of the Pharisees, as we see them so often trying to trick Our Lord into saying something incriminating (e.g. Luke 20:20). It can include petty spite and malice from family members, the proverbial nagging mother-in-law (Luke 12:53). And by analogy it can include all the woes and suffering brought on the world, by the world, by the wickedness of men or the ravages of outraged nature (Matth. 24:7).

When any of these evil things happen, we need not be surprised, for they were so clearly predicted in the Gospels. Instead we are told to rejoice – why? because the fact that they happen to us proves that we are among the strong ones of the faith, those who are capable of resisting, and who will not surrender our integrity in the face of attack. The weak need more protection – if we notice that we are somehow preserved from the disasters that happen to other people, and are conscious of the shielding wings behind us, we need the humility to admit it is because we are so feeble that we would not be able to cope with real suffering. There may yet be a place for us in heaven – but the place for the strong is "great in heaven." Those are the ones we call the hero saints, the martyrs.

Coming safely through the persecution does not, of course, mean surviving in this world, any more than it did for Our Lord Himself. Yet His death on the Cross was seen as His triumph, His glorification. He prayed that the Will of His Father be done, and "He was heard for His godly fear". (Heb. 5:7) In the same way the death of the martyrs is celebrated as their triumph, and made an occasion of joy in the Church on earth. God has delivered them from evil – He has set them free from doubt and uncertainty, and enabled them to confront evil face to face, and to conquer.

Amen!

We conclude all our prayers with that Hebrew word that is so often preserved by the Gospel writers upon Our Lord's lips, *amen*, "truth". It is one He uses to introduce some of His most important teaching. To be precise, seven times in the first three Gospels He says "Amen, I say unto you", and no less than twenty five times in St John's Gospel, "Amen, amen, I say unto you ..." (but the RSV translates it "truly, truly" and so loses the connection). Jesus Himself is called "The Amen" (Apoc. 3:14), because He is the Truth (John 14:6), and He came to bear witness to the Truth (John 18:37). "That they may know thee the only true God, and Jesus Christ whom thou hast sent." (John 17:3) It is of His very nature to be, and He is the source of being, for all that is came to be through Him (John 1:3).

We may say "Amen" because we wish to assent to what we have heard and affirm that it is the truth. Or we may say it as a wish, "let it be so" (as the French used to translate it, *ainsi soit-il*). We say it at the end of a prayer recited on our behalf by someone else, because we wish to associate ourselves with that prayer and to wish for everything contained in the prayer. We say it at the end of the Creed because we wish to affirm that the facts recited in the Creed are true – and maybe also we would like to pray for the faith to be able to say "I believe" and mean it. "I believe; help my unbelief!" (Mark 9:24) We say it at the end of a prayer we have ourselves recited, to confirm and ratify everything that has gone before.

The word does not, of course, come into the Gospel text of the Our Father in either version, but instinctively we use it to conclude the Prayer whenever we recite it. Oddly the exception is in the Mass, where the Our Father is followed immediately by the expanded prayer for protection from evil. Even in the classic Mass the "Amen" is only said silently, by the priest alone, for the choir gives its assent to the Our Father by joining in the last petition, *sed libera nos a malo*. For many centuries it was the custom for the Our Father to be recited only by the priest at Mass, or by the abbot at Vespers, on behalf of all present, who expressed their assent just with that last petition. (The reading from St Augustine used in the Divine Office on the last day before Advent, *Sermon* 256, 1-3, illustrates precisely this custom, "I go on to add, because of the perils still to come: 'Lead us not into temptation.' But how can the congregation be in security when it cries with me: 'Deliver us from evil.' ") Sometimes most of the Prayer was recited in silence, apart from the first and last words. Such a practice, universal until a generation ago, now seems strange, for we have become accustomed to think of the Our Father as essentially a community prayer, to be recited in unison by everyone present, whether at Mass or in the Divine Office or in any other form of public prayer. So indeed it is: we affirm our common Sonship, the fact that we are all children of our Father. But, for most of the history of the Church, that was expressed in a different way, and we should not condemn all our ancestors too easily, for whichever way the Prayer is said or sung, it is always the Prayer of the entire Church, precisely because it is the Prayer of Our Lord. Every phrase of the Lord's Prayer is found elsewhere in the Gospels on Our Lord's own lips, and all are echoed in the one great "priestly prayer" of Our Lord at the Last Supper. (John 17)

Whenever we pray the "Our Father", Christ prays in us, and we pray as members of the Church, the mystical Body of Christ living in the world. Whether we are alone in a remote place, or one of a vast crowd singing together in the Piazza of St Peter, we pray as one body, and that Prayer is certain to be answered, for in those words which the Son of God gave us, the Holy Spirit prays within us, and so we are united to the Father.

CHAPTER VI

The bridle as well

St Bernard somewhere tells the story of a richly caparisoned knight who was riding through the fields when he met a poor beggar. The beggar ranted against the knight, his fine horse and all its jingling harness, so the knight said, "I will give you the horse, if you can say just one Our Father without being distracted." "Easy," said the beggar, "Our Father, ... who art in heaven, ... hallowed be thy name, ... thy Kingdom ... do I get the bridle as well?"

Can any of us claim that we get even as far as that without being distracted? Our minds are utterly crammed with thoughts and memories and ideas, and they all come bubbling up to the surface the moment we set ourselves to pray. And the more we try to banish these distractions, the more insistently they come crowding back.

The first and greatest commandment is to love the Lord our God with all our heart and all our soul and all our might. How can we begin to claim that we love

Someone when we cannot keep our mind on Him for a minute at a time? The characteristic of being in love is that we can't *stop* thinking about the one we love; we find endless opportunities to bring their name into every conversation, we see the letters of their name in every possible anagram, we see everything in the context of the beloved, hear their voice in every phrase. Those are the common symptoms of being in love – and do we feel like that about God? Can we pass an instant without thinking of Him? Or can we, all too easily, go for hours without remembering Him at all, even though we do, really and honestly, wish to want to listen to Him?

When St Mary Magdalen sat quietly at the feet of Jesus and listened to Him speaking, when she stood below the cross to share His agony, when she wept for Him in the garden, was her mind distracted by a thousand little commonplace thoughts? Or was she intent on Him, fixed on Him, conscious of nothing other than Him?

Are we in love with God? Put like that, it is the most devastating examination of conscience possible: whatever else we do in life, no matter how we toil for the good of humanity, however fervent our preaching, or loud our hymn-singing, if we cannot even keep our thoughts on God for five minutes at a stretch, what sort of love is that?

Fortunately for us, there is a great difference between "being in love" and really loving. The common disease of "being in love" can often lead on to marriage, and family life, and fifty years or more of cooking and breadwinning and cleaning and nappy-changing and home-making, not without the occasional throwing of pots and pans and slamming of doors. After fifty years a couple can be seen to be deeply and truly loving, grown into each other so that neither is complete without the other, but the sparkle and the superficial glitter of "being in love" has long ago given place to something altogether more lasting and deeper. Few can experience "being in love with God" for very long, but we all can have a share, eventually, in the deep and transcendent love of God that cuts through all distractions, and overcomes all our stubborn reluctance to pray. After fifty years or more of trying to pray, trying to keep the commandments, trying to listen to the word of God, there may not be the glamour and the glitter – there may never have been – but the real deep love of God is there in the heart.

Prayer is not about feelings of love, it is about being, truly and literally, *in* Love, living in Him in whom we have our being. It occupies the whole of heart and might, and in an odd way, despite distractions, it can occupy the whole mind too. Everything that flits through the mind in prayer, no matter how irrelevant or irreverent it may seem, can be caught up into our love of God. Nothing is wasted. Above all we should never let our feelings in prayer deter us from persevering in prayer, for God listens to our prayer even when we don't.

Distraction and Detachment

Perhaps the real reason why our minds flitter around so much during prayer is that we have spent such a large proportion of our lives filling them with information, most of it quite useless. When we relax, all the pent-up ideas in the mind come bubbling up to the surface, and prayer is, after all, meant to be a relaxation from the bustle of daily life. We should not therefore be surprised at these distractions, nor unduly alarmed. In fact the more profound our state of prayer, the more likely it is that distracting thoughts will surface.

From our earliest childhood, we have been absorbing information through the senses. We see and hear so much, as we explore the world around us, long before anyone began the long thankless task of education. There are so many things in our memory, mostly the things we were not supposed to remember. Children can memorise and repeat long passages of dialogues from a film or programme they have seen only once, even if they have difficulty remembering the twelve-times-table or the past perfect of *pouvoir*. Our minds are crammed with vast amounts of data, most of which will be of no use to us whatever in later life. At school they expected us to learn the principal exports of Rhodesia, and the names of the great rivers of the Soviet Union, but it was somehow far easier to remember the names of the rivers of Narnia and the Thirteen Companions of Thorin Oakenshield. After leaving school we find that we cannot remember in the least how to do trigonometry, but we can recite the names of the whole class we joined when we were ten. Our minds are cluttered up with facts and figures, scenes and scents, such a quantity of information, all jumbled up together, useful and useless alike. And if in adult life we find that Rhodesia and the Soviet Union are no more, that metrication has made the twelve-times-table redundant; and no living Frenchman ever uses the past perfect tense, we can still remember the names of Balin and Dwalin and Bifur and Bombur, and waste ages trying to remember the rest of them. All that information is still swirling around in there somewhere, and it is quite likely to surface during prayer, when we are trying to think about God.

Why is this? It is because in profound prayer the real work is going on at a much deeper level than the conscious mind. You can call that deeper level what you like: some classical spiritual writers call it the "summit" or "apex" of the soul, others the "base"; moderns may call it the "subconscious" or the "unconscious". Newman called it the "illative sense". I prefer the Biblical term "heart". But whatever its name, it is that part of ourselves that is capable of perceiving God. Contact with God, the perception of God, is something intrinsically natural to all human beings, if only we knew it. But that contact is not, in itself, a matter of definite words, images or ideas; it is something much simpler, because God is essentially simple. The conscious rational mind has nothing to do during prayer, and that is why it wanders around all over the place, looking for something to devour. Abbot Chapman wrote a very perceptive analysis of this process, in an article, "What is Mysticism?", afterwards appended to the second edition of his *Spiritual Letters*.

Prayer is not altogether different from the process of sleep: the conscious mind is unoccupied, and amuses itself with confused memories and pictures which we call dreams. We should not be surprised if prayer and sleep are similar, nor in the least bit embarrassed if one should naturally lead into the other. Prayer, as I said, is meant to be relaxing. At the end of a busy day in the service of God, prayer is an opportunity to fall into our Father's arms. What father would be cross if his child fell asleep in his arms? Prayer is in fact the best possible way of preparing for sleep. If on waking our first thoughts and movements are those of prayer, what better way is there of awakening?

The distractions are not in themselves very dangerous, indeed they can be positively useful. First of all, the very fact that we have been distracted in prayer is a great humiliation – but without humility we shall never enter the kingdom of heaven. Being aware of our own foolishness is a very important part of our spiritual progress. It would be extremely bad for us, really dangerous, if we thought we were "good at prayer", or found it easy to unite ourselves to God, heart and will. When we are forced to recognise that we are so fickle that we cannot keep our mind on God for more than a minute at a stretch, then there is a chance that grace can work in us. Yet the virtue of humility is immediately at risk when we discover that all the greatest saints have experienced the same problem with distractions. St Teresa of Avila writes, "as for my attention wandering while reciting the Divine Office, I confessed it to-day to Fray Domingo, who told me to take no notice of it. I ask you to do the same, for I believe the evil is incurable". (*Letters*, no. 400, Stanbrook edition 1924, Vol. IV, p. 221) We hear of St Philip Neri that "If you suffer from distractions, or waverings of thought, and seem to pray without any profit whatever, the holy father encourages you, bidding you continue to pray through the whole time which you are wont to give to the exercise; and do nothing else but gently recall your thoughts and drive away the imaginations, for in doing so you gain merit, and this is not to waste time, but actually to pray." (*School of St Philip*, 1850, p. 19) We are in good company when we are distracted in prayer.

Secondly, if we pause to think about where our thoughts have been wandering during our prayer time, it makes an excellent examination of conscience. So often the subject of our distractions was food, or women, or power; we have been planning a meal, or a holiday, or what we shall do when we are Pope. The wandering thoughts have been exploring the possibilities of gluttony or lust, anger, sloth or pride. Those are the sins we would be committing, were it not for the grace of God. There is no sin in the catechism that each of us would not commit, if we were ever to lose sight of grace, and cut ourselves off from God. The only conclusion we can come to is thanksgiving for that grace, that has preserved us from all those sins, or has forgiven us when we did commit them and keeps us from committing them again.

When we end a time of prayer that has been full of distractions, if we accept the useful humiliation, and acknowledge the grace that has preserved us from sin, we shall have passed a very fruitful time of prayer indeed. What we thought was distraction has turned out to be a valuable meditation. With God, you cannot lose.

But it is the silence in the heart of our prayer that is even more valuable. And that silence we cannot discern. The real work of prayer is an operation of the love of God upon the heart, and like all the best heart surgery is done under anaesthetic. We don't remember the moments of silent union: all we remember is the preliminary distractions, and the ones at the end of our prayer, just as all we remember of our trip to the operating theatre is the preliminaries and the recovery.

What happens in that stillness? And how long does it last? The fact that real prayer is something actually impossible to discern is the reason why the Greek word *mysterion* and its derivatives have come to be associated with prayer. *Mysterion* means, literally, a "secret". St Paul uses it in the simple sense of something which used to be a secret and now has been revealed; a point of doctrine which was unknown to Jews and Gentiles, but has been told to us by Christ, and is now ready to be preached. Later writers, like St Denis (*Mystical Theology*), used it in a slightly different sense, to mean what God reveals to us in a secret manner. "Mystical" prayer therefore means simply "prayer in secret". We remember that Our Lord tells us to pray in secret, "and your Father who sees in secret will reward you" (Matth. 6:6). Abbot Chapman's explanation of the term "mysticism" is simply that it is a direct communication between God and the human soul, made in a manner that cannot be discerned, and which we can only afterwards explain or communicate in a very clumsy way. Several of the great saints tell us that this type of prayer is of very short duration, a momentary touch of God. St Thomas Aquinas explains that this is because nothing can remain at the peak of perfection for very long. (St Bernard, *Sermons on the Canticle of Canticles*, Mount Melleray edition 1920, vol. II, note to page 286, quoting St Thomas, St Teresa and others)

When we wake from our prayer, the conscious mind may try to put our experience of God into words, or to describe it in images. It is usually done very clumsily, and we prefer to use ready-made words and images. If people try to describe what their prayer has been like, they usually fall back on images they already have in mind, because they have no other way to describe things. There is nothing in the mind that has not previously passed through the senses. Ezekiel described his impression of the Cherubim in terms of those great winged statues from Babylon you can see in the Pergamum Museum, because these statues were familiar to him. Jeremiah described his insights in terms of familiar everyday objects, like a plumb-line, or a basket of figs. More commonly people focus on a familiar religious image, a Crucifix or a Mother and Child; or rest in familiar words, the psalms, the prayers of the Mass, or the Lord's Prayer. We would find it difficult to answer if anyone asked us to tell them exactly what we have been doing or thinking during our half-hour of mental prayer. All we could remember would be the distractions of the first few minutes and the last; in between we could say nothing.

The nothingness, of course, is very far from being a negation. We are not interested in searching for oblivion, or trying to elude the cares and worries of the world by sinking into a comfortable blank. No – in the unknown silence of our prayer God communicates a great deal, but not in a way we can immediately assimilate. It is like a message sent electronically through the air. A long and complicated message, complete with pictures, can be transmitted across the world in a fraction of a second. It takes a perceptible time for it to appear on a screen, even longer to print it out, longer still to read it and take in what it means. In the same way, in the twinkling of an eye God can transmit to the soul a profound message of sublime truth, but it can take us years to assimilate it, and to understand it.

When St John of the Cross tells us, "if you wish to know everything, seek to know nothing" (on his drawing, "the Mount of Perfection"), he means quite simply that the more we struggle to find things out, the less success we will have. Once we relax and let God take control, the knowledge we desire will come into the heart secretly and silently. He is not, emphatically not, saying that we should *wish* to know nothing, but that we should *seek* to know nothing. If we try to work things out for ourselves, and imagine that in the cleverness of our research we can actually penetrate the realities of God, then we shall get nowhere. If we pause from the busyness of the world and allow God to speak, He will tell us everything.

In the same way, if we wish to have everything, we should seek to have nothing; if we wish to be everything, we should seek to be nothing. Our wish is to have and be everything: we achieve it by letting go and surrendering to the will of God, letting Him give us everything, and make us sharers in the fullness of His life.

Waiting for God

In St Luke's Gospel, immediately before the passage where Our Lord introduces the Our Father, we find the charming little story of His first visit to Martha and Mary, when they were still living in Galilee (Luke 10:38-42). Martha was "distracted with much serving", while Mary "sat at the LORD's feet and listened to His teaching." From the earliest days Christian writers have interpreted this story as an instruction about the value of prayer above action, and the fact that St Luke follows it with the Our Father shows that it was his intention we should so understand it.

Martha, then, is the "type" of the busy active life, Mary of the "contemplative". Many Christians have seen these as two separate vocations in the Church: "contemplation" is often imagined to be a special state, reserved for the very few, the chosen souls who can spend hours sitting at Our Lord's feet and listening to His teaching. Most of us accept the role of Martha, and despite Our Lord's rebuke, we are inclined to think the Marys are merely idle. In the sixteenth century the pampered courtiers, who did nothing all day but hunt, and hover around the king's ante-chambers chatting to the ladies, asserted that all monks and nuns were "idle", and so they destroyed the monasteries where men and women filled every moment of the day with prayer and manual labour. In the twentieth century young men and women were firmly discouraged from trying their vocations as monks or nuns, because it would be a "waste of their lives", and their parents firmly directed them towards useful active careers as telephone sanitisers or beauticians. Ever since the eighteenth century, there has been a strand in Christian thinking that undervalues prayer and discourages contemplation, largely, one suspects, because of a fundamental lack of faith. If we do not believe in a God who cares about His people, then indeed there is no point in prayer, but there is not much point in pretending to be Christians either. It is because we do believe, that we pray, even if it is only to echo the Gospel prayer, "I believe; help my unbelief!" (Mark 9:24)

In reality there has to be something of Martha and something of Mary in each one of us. On the fifteenth-century monumental brass to Dom Thomas Nelond, Prior of Lewes in Sussex (now in Cowfold), the inscription tells he was "Martha in the eyes of the world, but Mary in the mind of Christ." *Mundo Martha fuit, sed Christi mente Maria.* The strictest monasteries and convents all insist on the importance of "manual labour", some sort of physical work interspersed with the hours of prayer. The motto *Ora et labora*, "pray and work" is attributed to St Benedict. The proverb *laborare est orare*, "work is prayer" can only be attributed to the devil, who delights in promoting it as an excuse for avoiding prayer. Oddly it is virtually unknown for any Christian to use prayer as an excuse for avoiding work, while it is devastatingly common to cite work as a good reason for cutting out prayer. Maybe a better proverb would be *Orare humanum est, laborare diabolicum* – prayer is what makes us truly human, the necessity for work is ultimately the result of the Fall, and therefore of the devil. Not that God does not use our human work as a means of sanctification.

The common phrase "a contemplative vocation" or "a contemplative Order" can be misleading. "Contemplation", as we have seen, is a term used in the Catholic tradition for simple prayer without words or images, as opposed to discursive or vocal prayer. However not all members of "contemplative orders" practise contemplation. The Carthusians, for example, fill the day with a busy round of vocal prayers, reading, and manual work, leaving very little time for mental prayer of any kind. Many monks and secular priests who try their vocation as Carthusians come back complaining there was no time for prayer. Carmelites certainly have a strong tradition of contemplative silent prayer, but not all of them are able to pray in this way, and many confine themselves to repeated vocal prayers. St Teresa wrote with great appreciation about the elderly nun she knew who could never pray in any way other than by reciting the Our Father. The English Benedictines are usually considered to be an "active" congregation, associated with running boys' schools, but they have a strong tradition of writers on contemplation, notably Dom Augustine Baker and Dom John Chapman, and their successors, such as my old guide Dom Victor Farwell who never wrote anything but was certainly a contemplative.

Contemplation, meaning a particular type of prayer, is by no means confined to the professionals, and by no means excludes a useful active work for the benefit of

God's people. One might go further and say that the most effective active work is done by those who spend most time in prayer, while those who neglect prayer somehow don't seem to get much work done either. This is not only a consideration for monks and nuns: lay Catholics are equally called to work for the Kingdom of Heaven, and they need the balance of prayer and work in exactly the same way. Perhaps the most famous definition of contemplative prayer, "I look at Him and He looks at me" came not from a hermit, nun or friar, but from a married village blacksmith.

A student once asked Father Michael Hollings how long she should spend on prayer every day. He answered, "About half an hour is a good average. Unless, of course, you are exceptionally busy, in which case it should be an hour." The more important our work, the more we need the help of God. If we do make the time to pray, then the work goes quicker, and more efficiently. Without prayer we shall find the day slipping past in useless idleness, and the work will not be done at all.

This is true of ordinary secular work – it is much more true of apostolic work, whether by lay apostles or clerics. A famous book by Dom Jean-Baptiste Chautard, *The Soul of the Apostolate,* sounded the alarm about the way in which priests were cluttering up their day with busy activities, and neglecting prayer. In particular they were developing an obsession with running boys' clubs, organising sports and outings, and dismissing the Divine Office as a mediaeval waste of time. Chautard was writing in 1907. He was translated into English by

Thomas Merton in 1945, who added an introduction warning that American priests had gone even further down this path of "activism". In 2007, a hundred years later, Chautard's warning is still relevant: priests are not ordained to organise sports, call bingo numbers, or attend committee meetings. Priests are ordained to pray, to preach, to celebrate Mass and administer the sacraments. It is no surprise that the Church in the West has failed, if priests fail to visit the sick because they are so busy coaching table-tennis.

But all this applies just as much to the lay apostolate. When Blessed Frédéric Ozanam founded the Society of St Vincent de Paul, he expected them to meet weekly for a considerable period of prayer and spiritual reading, which would give them the grace needed for their practical physical hard work among the poor. If a conference of the SVP skimps the prayer and spiritual reading in order to rush on to "business", it will soon dwindle away. This struck me many years ago when I met the Ladies' Conference of the Eastbourne SVP, who spent a good half hour on reading the New Testament and reflecting on its meaning, before despatching the "business" very efficiently. I can think of other Conferences that were not so edifying. Frank Duff insisted that the structure of prayer at meetings of the Legion of Mary should never be changed, and the result is that they still pray well together, and still do good apostolic work. Styles of prayer may change, and the rule of "pray as you can and don't try to pray as you can't" still applies, but no form of apostolic activity can survive without prayer.

There is a peculiar value for the apostolate in the prayer of silence, in which nothing of ourselves intrudes to block the action of the Holy Spirit. Any form of vocal prayer, or discursive meditation, is our own work: valuable, yes, but it can get in the way of the Holy Spirit. Silent contemplation is simply opening ourselves to the work of God. In the words of the psalm, "Be still, and know that I am God." (Psalm 45 (46):10)

It is easy to say "be silent", but extremely difficult to be so. Silence is difficult enough to preserve even in externals. How difficult it is to sit still without fidgeting, whistling or generally shuffling around. But that is nothing compared to the difficulty of keeping interior silence. The mind seems to be full of thoughts and memories, tunes and refrains, irrelevant and irreverent ideas drifting ceaselessly around. As we have seen, it is only the surface of the mind that is cluttered up in this way. The day may teem with activity, and the mind be crammed with innumerable items of information we have heard, countless sensations we have gathered and ignored, still as soon as we relax and unwind all those thoughts come bobbing up to the surface. The depths of the mind, the heart, the apex of the soul, whatever you call it – there there is stillness and calm. As the U-boat commander Niemöller wrote, while in prison for resisting the Nazis, "should there be occasional rough weather and storms on the surface, at a diving depth of twenty metres there is total calm." (Quoted in W. Hooper, *CS Lewis Collected Letters*, II (2004), 353 n.) It is in the calm depths that God speaks to us, as He spoke to the prophet Elijah in the "still small voice" (I Kg. 19:12). Only in the depths, not in the surface of the mind, can we be aware of the voice of the Holy Spirit, crying "Abba, Father", and praying within us "in sighs too deep for words". (Rom. 8:15, 26).

What this means is that real contemplative prayer is virtually impossible to detect. Our part, all that we can do, is to put ourselves in God's way. Then He takes over. Because the deeper part of the soul is occupied with listening to Him speaking, there is nothing for the imagination, the surface of the mind, to do, which is why all these "distractions" compass us about like bees. As St Antony used to say, "only when you do not know you are praying can you be truly praying." We do not hear God's voice in the conscious mind – or at least it is extremely rare to hear Him thus – but He speaks directly to the soul. All we are aware of is the distracted surface, and that can be so irritating. That is why we may be tempted to dismiss the whole business as a total waste of time, and either take refuge in reading ready-made meditations, or abandon prayer in order to concentrate on running a youth club. It takes courage to go on "wasting time" with God. But it is, in truth, the most effective way of making our apostolate truly fruitful.

Appendix

Some Spiritual Classics

"Prefer to read books by authors whose names begin with St."
(St Philip Neri)

But there are some good authors who have not yet been canonised:

Anon, *The Cloud of Unknowing.*
    Philokalia: Early Fathers on Prayer of the Heart.
    The Way of a Pilgrim.
St Aelred of Rievaulx, *Mirror of Charity,*
                Spiritual Friendship.
St Augustine, *Confessions.*
Dom Augustine Baker, *Holy Wisdom.*
St Benedict, *Holy Rule.*
St Bernard, *Sermons on the Canticle of Canticles.*
Dom Louis de Blois (Blosius), *Comfort for the Faint-Hearted.*
St John Cassian, *Eight Deadly Sins,*
        Collations.
Père de Caussade, *Abandonment to Divine Providence.*
Dom John Chapman, *Spiritual Letters.*
Fr Walter Ciszek, *He Leadeth Me.*
Dom Jean-Baptiste Chautard, *The Soul of the Apostolate.*
St Denis, *Mystical Theology.*

St José-Maria Escriva, *The Way*.

Fr F W Faber, *Growth in Holiness*.

St Francis of Assisi, *The Little Flowers*.

St Francis de Sales, *Introduction to the Spiritual Life, Treatise on the Love of God*.

St Gregory the Great, *Pastoral Care*.

St Gregory of Nyssa, *Life of Moses*.

Père Jean Grou, *How to Pray*.

Walter Hilton, *The Scale of Perfection*.

St John of the Cross, *The Ascent of Mount Carmel*.

St Julian of Norwich, *Revelations*.

Bl. John Ruysbroeck, *The Sparkling Stone*.

Ven. Thomas à Kempis, *Imitation of Christ*.

Bl. Columba Marmion, *Christ in his Mysteries*.

Dom Thomas Merton, *Seeds of Contemplation*.

St Philip Neri, *Maxims*.

Richard of St Victor, *Benjamin Minor, Benjamin Major*.

Richard Rolle, *The Fire of Love*.

Lorenzo Scupoli, *The Spiritual Combat*.

Bl. Henry Suso, *Eternal Wisdom*.

St Teresa of Jesus, *The Way of Perfection*.

St Thérèse of the Child Jesus, *Autobiography*.

Bl. Teresa of Calcutta, *Come be my Light*.

St William of St Thierry, *Golden Epistle*.